PARTNERS IN STRATEGY:
RSLs, the local authority strategic role and the shape of the sector

A report for the Chartered Institute of Housing
sponsored by the Joseph Rowntree Foundation

By

Sarah Rowe with Celia Cashman and Jeff Zitron
HACAS Chapman Hendy

June 2001

The Chartered Institute of Housing

The Chartered Institute of Housing is the professional organisation for all people who work in housing. Its purpose is to maximise the contribution that housing professionals make to the well-being of communities. The Institute has more than 17,000 members working in local authorities, housing associations, government agencies, the private sector and educational institutions.

Chartered Institute of Housing
Octavia House
Westwood Way
Coventry CV4 8JP
Telephone: 024 7685 1700
www.cih.org

Partners in Strategy: RSLs, the local authority strategic role and the shape of the sector
A report for the Chartered Institute of Housing sponsored by the Joseph Rowntree Foundation.
By Sarah Rowe with Celia Cashman and Jeff Zitron, HACAS Chapman Hendy
Edited for CIH by Mark Lupton and John Perry

The Joseph Rowntree Foundation has supported this project as part of its programme of research and innovative development projects, which it hopes will be of value to policy makers, practitioners and service users. The facts presented and views expressed in this report, however, are those of the authors and not necessarily those of the Foundation.

© Chartered Institute of Housing 2001
Published by the Chartered Institute of Housing

ISBN 1 903208 10 6

Graphic design by Jeremy Spencer
Cover photograph by Jon Walter
Printed by Genesis Print & Marketing

Contents

Foreword

The Chartered Institute of Housing is a keen advocate of a stronger strategic housing role for local authorities and was pleased with the emphasis given to it in the Housing Green Paper. Jointly with the Local Government Association, we have called for a stronger legal basis for the strategic role. Again jointly with the LGA, we have published good practice guidance on how it should develop. And with the Council of Mortgage Lenders we have drawn attention to the need for local authorities to understand and, where necessary, influence the wider housing market in their areas. Our report *Sustaining Success* (also with HACAS) focussed on housing markets and their effect on RSLs in areas of low housing demand.

As part of this continuing attention to housing strategies, the current report looks in more detail at how the role of local authorities might develop in relation to the RSLs in their area, both as providers of new housing and as agents for community regeneration. It also raises the issue of the 'shape' of the social housing sector in an area, and whether and how councils might aim to 'reshape' it to aid the delivery of their strategies. We make extensive use of case study material from Manchester, Brent and the Welland Partnership in the East Midlands.

The report is being published both to influence developing Government policy in this field, and to draw attention to developing good practice. The relationships between local authorities and RSLs are critical to the success of housing strategies and we hope that the report may help to ensure that they are more focussed and more productive.

Chartered Institute of Housing

June 2001

Acknowledgements

The Chartered Institute of Housing and the authors would like to thank the many organisations and individuals that took part in and contributed to the study. In particular we would like to thank those who attended the workshop in December 2000.

Special thanks go to the case study authorities and RSLs for the time and energy they contributed to the project, and to the project advisory group which was:

Aman Davi
Mary Dyer
Robert Fox
Neil Haddon
Paul Lautman
Mike Morris
David Mullins
Andy Snowden
Janet Solomon
Eric Thomasson
Steve Wilcox
Peter Williams

CIH and HACAS Chapman Hendy would also like to thank the Joseph Rowntree Foundation for funding and supporting the project. We are particularly grateful to Alison Jarvis for her valuable input.

Executive summary

The Government's policy statement *The Way Forward for Housing* heralds big changes in the strategic housing role of local authorities. The Chartered Institute of Housing has already explored issues such as designing local housing strategies, understanding local housing markets, and the need for stronger legal powers and duties relating the wider strategic role. This report aims to explore in more detail how the wider role affects the relationships between councils and the registered social landlords operating in their areas and make proposals about how these should develop.

Study objectives

This study has involved an evaluation of two inter-related areas of housing policy:

- the Government's promotion of the local authority strategic housing role (and the latter's separation from the provider role), and;
- the changing shape and role of the social housing sector, as a consequence of factors such as large-scale voluntary transfer, the broadening (and increasingly cross-tenure remit) of many RSLs, and rent-restructuring.

The study has sought to explore the implications of these changes for the relationship between local authorities and the RSL sector.

Study method

The study involved the following:

- An initial workshop involving representatives of a range of interested agencies, and local authority representatives, to clarify the scope of the study and the range of available source materials.
- Case study visits to three areas (the London Borough of Brent, Manchester City Council and the Welland Partnership, an alliance of district councils and a unitary authority in the East Midlands). The case study areas were selected to provide an example of good practice in one or more aspects of the strategic housing role, whilst illustrating the diversity of the local authority sector and the range of contextual factors that impact upon the strategic housing role. A profile of each of the case study areas can be found in the appendices.
- Desk-based research, drawing together previous research reports and good practice guidance, and an evaluation of examples of good practice drawn from HACAS Chapman Hendy's client base.

The policy context for the study

Since the late 1990s there has been an increasing focus on the need for community leadership from local authorities, and on the need to involve a wide range of local stakeholders in identifying housing needs and planning responses. There has also been a growing emphasis on the need to ensure that housing strategy is considered alongside wider strategies to promote social inclusion and community sustainability.

This has implications for the relationship between RSLs and local authorities, as local authorities are being expected to intervene to influence the activities of RSLs in ways that extend beyond traditional forms of interaction.

Local authorities are also being encouraged to develop new approaches to assessing housing demand, in the context of local housing markets. Authorities need to address private market capacity alongside the functioning of the social housing sector, and to consider both within the wider context of community sustainability. An important driver in the focus on housing markets has been the impact of changing demand in some parts of the country, particularly the Midlands and the North.

The Government has made clear that it expects local authorities to play a stronger strategic role in all areas of their work. Local authorities are expected to embrace the role of champion of consumers in all housing sectors, private and public, and including the RSL sector.

There is an assumption that separating local authorities' strategic and provider roles will help to strengthen both. The DETR has said it will consider allowing local authorities a greater role in allocating social housing grant and monitoring RSLs where local authorities no longer provide housing, a policy already agreed in Scotland.

Questions have been asked about the extent to which local authorities are embracing new definitions of the strategic housing role. Indeed, research into LSVT authorities suggests that despite achieving a full split between the strategic and provider functions, many local authorities have not developed the strategic housing role in the way the Government expects.

The changing shape of the social housing sector

Current stock transfer programmes, combined with the impact of right to buy and trends in new provision, suggest that by 2005, RSLs will own more homes than local authorities. In addition RSLs are expected to tackle a much wider range of tasks than in the past. RSLs are also under pressure to increase the quality of their homes and services, but at the same time to reduce costs, principally in order to maintain rent affordability. The Government's new rent restructuring regime will increase these pressures, as rent levels for some RSLs in some areas may need to be reduced, and general rent rises are capped.

Gaining economies of scale and reducing duplication is an increasingly important issue for RSLs. And an increasingly common way of addressing these issues is through the development of a group structure.

The report provides an analysis of the way in which RSLs have approached the formation of group structures in recent years. Virtually all restructuring activity has been initiated by RSLs themselves; the Housing Corporation has traditionally been reluctant to broker RSL reorganisation, other than in rescue cases.

The Government and the Housing Corporation have been at the forefront of calls for the RSL sector to rationalise management. These calls reflect concerns that the sheer number of RSLs serving some communities, and the scatter of stock in some cases, does not make sense in terms of efficient management or meeting local needs.

There has been little public debate about what rationalisation might mean in practice; the term pre-supposes that a judgement can reasonably be made on what a "rational" structure for the sector looks like for an area. However, there are many unanswered questions, particularly in relation to the role of local authorities in defining the need for and facilitating change at a time of increasing RSL-generated merger activity. This report seeks answers to some of those questions.

The strategic housing role

In the study report, an analysis is provided of the way in which case study authorities deliver the strategic housing role. This analysis reveals a number of issues that would need to be addressed to support any move to create a statutory basis for the function. These issues include:

- how to address the needs of authorities, and in particular smaller authorities, that are not well placed to maintain a statutory strategic role in isolation from the provider role
- how to address the resource implications of expanding the strategic role.

The report suggests ways that these issues might be addressed.

The relationship between local authorities and RSLs

The new demands of the strategic housing role have wide-ranging implications for the relationship between local authorities and RSLs, arising in particular from the expectation that authorities will intervene to influence the capacity and operation of the RSL sector. As the Housing Corporation is itself responsible for ensuring that RSLs achieve appropriate performance standards and consult and involve their customers, this implies that a re-appraisal of the respective roles of and the relationship between local authorities and the Housing Corporation will be needed.

The report provides an analysis of the way in which case study authorities currently seek to influence the operation of the sector. Approaches include:

- conditions attached to the allocation of grant (which in Manchester and Brent will now be handled through a joint commissioning process with the Housing Corporation)
- promotion of best practice, through liaison and consultation with RSLs
- special requirements for large scale voluntary transfer RSLs, involving performance monitoring as a requirement of contract and Board Membership for local authority nominees.

The study found that each of the case study organisations has to a greater or lesser degree sought or intends to seek to influence standards of management practice amongst RSLs. There is also an agenda to obtain "added value" through the commissioning process for partner RSLs. However, the roles and responsibilities of local authorities and the Housing Corporation in influencing RSL performance need to be addressed.

The report proposes a series of principles to govern the relationship between local authorities and the Housing Corporation, assuming a greater degree of local authority influence in monitoring the operation of the sector.

Influencing the capacity and shape of the RSL sector

The report examines case study authorities' views on the need and scope for intervention to influence the shape of the sector:

- In Brent, there is no formal agenda to seek rationalisation of the stock. The authority has however actively promoted the transfer of newly-developed homes to BME RSLs, and views diversity of provision as an essential feature of the sector. The authority wishes to preserve some flexibility within its joint commissioning arrangements for bids from non-partner agencies.

- In Manchester, rationalisation of the sector is viewed as important to underpin the delivery of corporate housing strategy, with its focus on cross-tenure approaches to addressing problems with housing markets and community sustainability. However the council is clear that its ability to influence the shape of the sector is ultimately dependent on the Housing Corporation.

- Whilst the Welland Partnership has not developed a formal strategic position on rationalisation, officers believe that there may be value in exploring the need for/benefits of rationalisation. Officers felt that any such debate would need to be based upon a willingness on the local authority side, as well as the RSL side, to give up the management of stock where this is in the interests of communities and efficient management.

Views on the need for rationalisation vary considerably, reflecting to a degree the extent to which intervention in the market is perceived as necessary to deliver strategic objectives.

It is questionable whether local authorities will be able, successfully, to carry out the strategic housing role as it is now defined without fully understanding the profile of the sector, and considering the extent to which landlords, individually and as a whole, are capable of meeting local requirements. This implies that local authorities should have a role in influencing the shape and operation of the sector (in addition to an understanding of how RSLs are performing).

The report suggests mechanisms for authorities and RSLs to develop approaches that suit the needs of their communities, and cautions against relying on unspoken or ill-defined notions of "rational" ownership or management. Given the independence of the RSL sector, and the consensus for partnership working, such mechanisms need to be collaborative. However, local authorities, the Housing Corporation and RSLs all need to recognise that some "teeth" are likely to be needed, particularly inasmuch as each is genuinely committed to giving tenants and other consumers a real say.

The report outlines three alternative models for proactive intervention, and the capacity of each model for increasing local authorities' ability to influence the work of the RSL sector in order to better carry out the strategic and enabling roles. It concludes that a "managed market approach" which is essentially based upon collaboration, but supported by the available statutory and contractual powers, should enable local authorities to intervene more effectively to deliver the strategic role.

The managed market approach needs to include a more effective evaluation of the profile and capacity of the RSL sector, and greater collaboration between local authorities and the Housing Corporation in evaluating the capacity of the sector and influencing outcomes. This would have the benefit of respecting the independence of the RSL sector, whilst equipping local authorities to be more active in overseeing the sector's management in partnership with the Housing Corporation.

Conclusions and recommendations

A statutory definition

There is a strong case for creating a statutory basis for the strategic housing role. However, legislation needs to be underpinned by greater clarity about what that role entails, and linked to a clearer understanding of how it will be resourced.

The meaning of the strategic/provider split

The Government has suggested that it may consider allowing local authorities that have transferred their stock to assume greater responsibilities in respect of the RSL sector. Government needs to clarify its expectations on this issue, and the implications for local authorities that do not transfer their housing stock. Clarity on this issue is important to underpin the debate on resourcing the role, and establishing a statutory requirement; local authorities that have achieved full separation could, for example, be offered financial support to resource the strategic role, and assume responsibilities (and access to regulatory information on the RSL sector) which might not otherwise be available.

Resourcing the role

There is a resource implication in expanding the strategic role that needs to be addressed. One option would be to review revenue support grant provision to local authorities, to reflect the new demands of the strategic role. Any review of RSG should be linked to a clear statement of the role itself, and the outcomes that Government expects local authorities to achieve.

Alternatives to local authority delivery

For some authorities it may be necessary to consider alternative methods of delivery. Options include:

- Local authorities could be given the power to delegate any statutory function to an external agency (including ones formed as joint ventures with partners) in order to facilitate social and economic regeneration.
- Local authorities that have transferred their housing stock could be permitted to create a strategic housing service with neighbouring LAs; DETR should provide funding for a pilot programme.

Clarifying the statutory requirements

The LGA and CIH have produced a series of recommendations on the nature of the obligations that should be enforceable through statute. We recommend that these requirements are extended, as detailed in chapter 3, and are accompanied by new obligations for RSLs and Regional Development Agencies.

The relationship to the social housing sector

There is a strong case for local authorities being able to influence the shape and capacity of the social housing sector, in collaboration with other key stakeholders (including tenants and leaseholders and the Housing Corporation) as part of their wider responsibility for ensuring the effective operation of the local housing market. This is particularly important at a time when the sector is experiencing a period of rapid change.

This would involve the "managed market approach" to using the powers that are currently available, and would be based upon collaboration between local authorities, RSLs and the Housing Corporation. Specifically we recommend that:

- Given the significant and increasing role that RSLs are playing in delivering local authority strategies, local authorities should be required (say) every 3-5 years to prepare an RSL sector "Expectations Statement" – detailing what is needed from the sector.
- Together, locally operating RSLs and local authorities should produce a "Capacity Statement" identifying what the sector can deliver locally and how any gaps can be filled.
- The Housing Corporation should provide funding for this process and act as "auditor" of the Capacity Statement. Local authorities should be encouraged to undertake this exercise jointly with other local authorities.

Local authorities as consumer champions

Authorities should ensure that RSL tenants have full access to opportunities for involvement and participation. This should include:

- providing opportunities for RSL tenants' participation in Community and Housing Strategy development (in collaboration with RSLs)
- encouraging RSLs to consult their tenants effectively, and monitoring their performance in this respect
- working with RSLs to establish shared consultation arrangements in multi-landlord communities.

To ensure that there is a local lever for effective management, RSL tenants should have the right to initiate a review by the Housing Corporation of the management of their homes by their RSL. This could be linked to the Best Value inspection regime. This would be triggered by a minimum number or proportion of an RSL's tenants in a local authority area demonstrating (by reference to the performance of the RSL) that the service to them did not reach an acceptable standard, and the RSL failing to address this satisfactorily within a given timescale. The results of such a review would be published, including any recommendations, which could include proposals for the management of the homes to be transferred to another RSL. This could be mirrored by an equivalent right for local authority tenants to initiate an inspection by the Housing Inspectorate.

The roles of the Housing Corporation and local authorities

Any development of the local authority strategic function has implications for the role of the Housing Corporation. Further consideration therefore needs to be given to the relationship between the Housing Corporation and local authorities, and particularly to information sharing arrangements. In chapter 4, the report sets out principles to underpin the redefinition of relationships.

LA monitoring role

Local authorities should address the need to promote best practice, and Best Value, amongst all providers of social housing in the area. This should include developing/preferred partner RSLs as well as non-partner/non-developing RSLs, and also local authority owned providers.

For developing RSLs this should focus on how they perform in delivering the outputs and outcomes required by funding/partnership agreements (and should be fully integrated with Corporation monitoring arrangements). The extent of local authority responsibility in this respect could be linked to the extent of separation from the provider function. A second regime could operate for all RSLs including non-developing RSLs. We would endorse the suggestion from some RSLs involved in this study that such monitoring should focus on broad outcomes such as customer satisfaction with housing services, and should draw on the standard performance information data that RSLs are now required to produce. A challenge for all social housing providers will be to disaggregate data to neighbourhood level, to allow for an examination of the way that communities are served.

1 Introduction

Aims of the study

This study has evaluated two inter-related areas of policy:

- The Government's intention to promote the development of local authorities' strategic housing role, to ensure that authorities address the housing and related needs of all consumers, and link housing strategy with wider plans for improving the social, economic and environmental well-being of the community. The principal objective of this study has been to examine the implications of this change for the relationship between local authorities and RSLs, and to examine, why, whether and how the relationship between them needs to change. In order to provide a context for this analysis, the study has also explored local authorities' perceptions of the strategic housing role, and the constraints they face in seeking to embrace new definitions of the role.

- The second area of examination, very much linked to the first, is the implications of the changing shape of the social housing sector, for local authority relationships with RSLs. There have been calls for RSLs to rationalise management arrangements for their stock, where for example, they own small numbers of properties at some distance from a management base. There have also been suggestions that there are too many RSLs operating in some areas. The study has examined the ways in which local authorities seek to influence the operation of the RSL sector, and also asked whether (and how) local authorities should intervene to influence the shape of the sector. It should be emphasised that whilst the interaction between strategic housing authorities and RSLs has been the focus of the study, this is just one aspect of the wider strategic housing role, which local authorities should address in the round.

We consider the context for these policy initiatives in chapter 2.

A considerable body of work has been developed in recent years to define and provide guidance on the strategic housing function. Recent examples of this work include:

- a survey of local authorities' views on the strategic housing role, and the nature of their strategic activities, carried out by the LGA in November 2000. Of the 376 local authorities providing strategic housing services in England and Wales, 245 responded to the survey (65%) (LGA, 2001)

- a CIH/LGA review of the legislative basis for the strategic housing role (CIH/LGA, 2001)

- a report by the IPPR looking at the future of social housing, which included an analysis of the need for a stronger strategic role for local authorities (IPPR, 2000)

- a report by the LGA task group looking at the future strategic housing role of local authorities, in the context of the government's modernisation agenda, the strengthening of local authorities' community leadership role, and the strategies for promoting social inclusion (LGA, 2000)

- good practice guidance on designing local housing strategies (CIH/LGA, 1998) and on developing rural housing strategies (CIH/The Countryside Agency/The Housing Corporation, 2000).

The last year has also seen the publication a number of documents that have relevance to specific aspects of the strategic housing function including:

- guidance on the assessment of housing need (DETR, 2000c)
- guidance on the role of local housing markets in housing strategies (CIH/CML, 2000)
- good practice guidance on tackling low demand and unpopular housing (DETR, 2000e).

In addressing questions about the definition and breadth of an expanded strategic housing role, we have drawn on and greatly benefited from this existing body of work. Our intention in conducting this study has been to add value to what has gone previously. We have done this by building upon and developing the definitions provided by previous studies and by recommending practical ways of addressing the constraints that authorities face in delivering the strategic housing role. However, as noted above, the central focus of our work has been the implications of an expanded strategic role for local authority relationships with RSLs, and whether there is a role for local authorities in influencing the capacity and shape of the sector in any given area.

This study has focussed upon the English context, and does not address the obligations of Welsh and Scottish local authorities, or the profile of the social housing sector in Wales and Scotland. However, it should be noted that both the Welsh Assembly and the Scottish Executive envisage a more strategic role for housing authorities, alongside changes to the framework for housing investment in both countries.

Structure of the report

The remaining sections of chapter 1 deal with the way we carried out the research for the study, and provide some definitions of the terms used.

The following chapters of the report deal with the two related elements of the study (the strategic role, and its relationship to the social housing sector) as follows:

- **Chapter 2** provides an evaluation of the policy background for our analysis of the strategic housing role, highlighting the national policy context, the way that the Government wishes local authorities to change, the way the shape of the social housing sector is changing and the debate about the need for rationalisation of the sector, and the role that local authorities might play in this.

- **Chapter 3** examines the nature of the strategic housing role, the way in which case study authorities interpret and carry out the role (with an emphasis on intelligence gathering, and cross-border partnerships), and the case for enforcing the role in statute. It also examines the constraints that need to be addressed to enable more authorities to embrace the new approach.

- **Chapter 4** examines the relationship between local authorities and the RSL sector, and the implications of new definitions of the strategic housing role for the relationship, drawing on case study evidence, and examines the need for new approaches.

- **Chapter 5** looks at the reasons why local authorities should intervene in the sector, and a range of different models for local authority intervention.

The way the study was carried out

Our research has involved the following:

a) An initial workshop involving representatives of a range of interested agencies, and local authority representatives, to clarify the scope of the study and the range of available source materials.

b) Case study visits to three areas (the London Borough of Brent, Manchester City Council and the Welland Partnership, an alliance of district councils & a unitary authority in the East Midlands). The case study areas were selected to provide an example of good practice in one or more aspects of the strategic housing role, whilst illustrating the diversity of the local authority sector and the range of contextual factors that impact upon the strategic housing role.

c) Desk-based research, drawing together previous research reports and good practice guidance, an evaluation of examples of good practice drawn from HACAS Chapman Hendy's client base and an evaluation of the national policy context.

The case studies

The case studies involved a combination of desk-based research, to evaluate written sources of information from the local authorities (including strategy documentation and HIP returns), and interviews with officers (and in one area with the lead member for housing).

In Brent and Manchester, interviews were conducted with senior local authority officers from the housing service, and with officers of 4-6 RSLs of a range of sizes and types with active development programmes in the relevant local authority area.

In the Welland Partnership area, we approached the evaluation from the perspective of one of the partner authorities, Rutland County Council, as well as considering the Partnership-wide approach to the strategic process. The desk-based evaluation included an analysis of documents for Rutland County Council, as well as for the Partnership as a whole. Interviews were conducted with senior officers from four of the five Partnership authorities (Harborough District Council, Melton Borough Council, Rutland County Council and South Kesteven District Council). Discussions were also held with three RSLs operating in the Partnership area.

Key issues for the case studies included:

- officers' views on what the strategic function entails
- the way that the strategic housing role is delivered
- the extent to which enabling activities are provided on a cross-tenure basis
- the way that partnerships with RSLs and others are managed
- approaches to customer involvement
- approaches to intelligence gathering to support the strategic planning process
- the way that authorities are responding to the changing national and regional context (taking account of influences such as the neighbourhood renewal agenda and the priorities of the new regional chambers/assemblies).

The case study evaluations involved a wide-ranging review of the work that authorities have been doing to deliver particular aspects of the enabling role, including stock transfer activity, intervention in the private rented sector and activities to support home owners. The coverage of each of the case study reports varies, reflecting the diverse contexts within which each authority or group of authorities operates. A profile of each of the case study areas can be found in the Appendices. Where relevant, material from the case studies has also been included in the body of the report. Full transcripts of each case study report are separately available from the Chartered Institute of Housing through the Choice for Housing website (www.c4h.org).

Advisory group

The study has also been overseen by an advisory group, established by the Joseph Rowntree Foundation, which funded this project. Advisory group members are listed at the front of this document, and have contributed both in scoping the study and reviewing the draft report. The views contained in the study do not necessarily represent those of advisory group members or their organisations.

Terminology and definitions

Throughout the report we use the term "registered social landlord" (RSL) to refer to housing associations, local housing companies and housing co-operatives that are registered with the Housing Corporation.

We use the term "social housing" to refer to rented or shared ownership housing provided at below market cost by local authorities or RSLs. We use the term "low-cost market housing" to refer to private sector provision at the cheapest end of the local housing market. The term affordable housing is used to refer to both social housing and low-cost market housing.

The term "private sector agencies" is used as a general term to refer to the full range of agencies operating in the private sector including private landlords and developers, lenders, estate agents, and businesses.

The term local housing market is also used throughout the report, to refer to the entire housing market in any given area, including privately rented and owner occupied housing. Local housing markets may operate across local authority boundaries, and the presumption throughout this report is that local authorities should develop their understanding of the way markets operate, even where these extend beyond administrative boundaries.

The strategic housing function

An important element of this study has been to develop a detailed definition of what the strategic housing function entails and how it can be delivered. These definitions are considered in more depth in chapter 3. But it is useful to note here the description of the strategic housing role that was used in the Housing Green Paper (DETR, 2000a), as this has provided the starting point for our analysis:

"The main strands of an authority's strategic role for housing are:

1) *Assessing the needs of local communities, balancing those needs with national priorities, and producing a clear strategy for tackling problems across all types of housing in the area, based on consultation*

2) Identifying, co-ordinating and facilitating all the resources and agencies that can contribute to the delivery of the strategy

3) Co-ordinating and planning for the provision and development of additional housing, both in the private and social sectors, helping to create sustainable communities

4) Acting as a service provider (including the administration of lettings schemes and housing benefit) and commissioning housing and services from other agencies as appropriate

5) Linking housing with wider policies for the social, economic and environmental well-being of the area, including the regeneration of deprived neighbourhoods

6) Operating and facilitating local partnership schemes to encourage best practice amongst providers of housing and housing services

7) Enforcing and raising standards

8) Consulting and empowering the local community

9) Providing and commissioning advice and assistance, for example to help homes people to find suitable housing

10) Taking action to tackle anti-social behaviour, including racial harassment, across all tenures

11) Working with neighbouring authorities and other agencies to meet housing need and tackle housing problems across wider areas in the region

12) Monitoring and evaluating the success of the strategy and revising it where necessary."

The enabling role

The terms "enabling" and "strategic" have frequently been used on an interchangeable basis. Much of the literature of the early-mid 1990s focussed on local authorities as enablers, describing a role which is closely related to the strategic role described above. For example, *Vision into reality – the role of transfer authorities as housing enablers* describes the enabling role as:

- developing a comprehensive housing strategy for the area which itself incorporates strategies for investment, housing and community care planning

- securing the delivery of the strategy

- facilitating co-operation between services and other agencies

- securing the delivery of services for which the authority is responsible either directly or through other agents

- influencing and developing the market for local authority services

- developing influence outside these services in circumstances where this would contribute to the local authority's strategic objectives (Aldbourne Associates, 1997).

However, whilst the terms "enabling" and "strategic" have been used interchangeably, and clearly have elements of overlap, we have sought to distinguish between the two. In our view the enabling functions can usefully be understood as the activities needed to deliver the strategic role. Consequently, for the purposes of this study, we draw on the dictionary definitions of the two terms: the strategic role involves putting in place the overall policy framework and action plan for achieving objectives and targets, whilst the enabling functions are those which deliver the strategy.

Partnerships

The term "partnership" can be used to refer to a wide range of relationships between local authorities and other stakeholders and agencies, including formal liaison arrangements, contractual agreements and joint ownership. We have therefore avoided using the term, unless we are referring in the most general terms to any form of relationship between agencies. In the following table we provide definitions for the variety of arrangements that are available to authorities to deliver housing strategy.

Figure 1: Options for delivery of strategic and enabling roles

Method	Definition	LA's form of influence and control
Direct provision	LA staff deliver – largely or wholly alone	Direct management and deployment of resources
Outsourced provision	LA retains client role – service provided by external agent	Contractual rights
Funding	External agency produces agreed output (e.g. affordable housing) for specified funding (e.g. grant or free land). Whilst LA may retain some rights (e.g. nominations or referrals) there is no long term client/agent relationship	Allocation and payment of grants; scheme scrutiny; standard setting
Joint planning/delivery arrangement	Liaison with other agencies (inc. service level agreements)	Choice of partners; commissioning of research; form of agreement; monitoring and enforcement procedures
Joint planning/delivery contract	Contractual arrangement with other agencies (legally binding) to deliver agreed outputs/services. Delivery is through one or more of the parties to the contract so client/agent relationship maintained.	Contractual rights
Joint venture delivery vehicle	LA jointly owns (and may jointly manage) legal entity with other partner. Likely to mean greater sharing of risk/reward than other models. (e.g. equity investment).	Ownership rights e.g. to elect the board. May be proportionate to level of investment (as in commercial company) or based on agreed governance model (as in RSL). Management rights – agreement and implementation of business plan
Information/voluntary guidance/ encouragement/ exhortation	Researching, making available information for use by others, disseminating and supporting good practice	Affected by extent of other influences over "audience" (e.g. grant giving powers) and by general political influence
Transfer responsibility to other LA service	Housing service no longer has responsibility but remains within LA's ambit.	Will depend on which of the above methods is used to influence/control
Transfer responsibility to other agency	LA no longer has responsibility	Depends on "exit strategy" e.g. is passing over of responsibility based on future right to be consulted?

These terms are used throughout the report where relevant.

Local strategic partnerships (LSPs)

The Government has recently published guidance on LSPs (DETR, 2001c). The Government anticipates that LSPs will be initiated by local authorities, and will involve agencies from all relevant sectors (public, private and voluntary). Any of the partner agencies may take the lead role in facilitating and steering the partnership, but the Government expects to see local authority member involvement.

The role of LSPs is to:

- prepare & implement community strategy
- provide a forum through which public service providers work together effectively
- link to local public service agreements where these exists
- deliver local neighbourhood renewal strategy.

The Government suggests that LSPs are likely to have the following characteristics:

- they are aligned with local authority boundaries
- they bring together public/private/business/community/voluntary sectors
- they are non-statutory and non-executive
- they enable strategic decisions to be taken and be close enough to individual neighbourhoods to allow actions to be determined at community level.

Whilst guidance envisages alignment with local authority boundaries, our research suggests that authorities are already considering the formation of cross-border LSPs, either to address the needs of a sub-region that encompasses more than one authority, or to serve a neighbourhood that crosses the border of two or more authorities (but is contained within them). Where the term LSP is used, we have not presumed that the partnership will be aligned with a single local authority.

2 The changing national context

Introduction

In this section of the report we examine three key elements of the changing national context:

1. changing definitions of the strategic housing role
2. the implications of this change for relationships between strategic housing authorities, RSLs, and the Housing Corporation
3. the changing profile of the social housing sector, and the questions that this raises about the extent to which local authorities should be involved in influencing the shape of the sector.

Changing definitions of the strategic housing role

The expectation that local authorities should operate as enablers, intervening to meet housing need on a cross tenure basis and working with partners in the private and public sectors, is not new. Since the 1988 Housing Act, local housing authorities have been expressly urged to embrace the enabling and co-ordinating role, and to develop partnerships with housing associations, voluntary and private sector agencies to meet housing need (see for example HMSO, 1987; DoE, 1994). However, perceptions of the enabling role have changed, alongside changes in the role of local authorities and the economic and social context within which they operate.

The new strategic housing role has been influenced by the following:

a) An increasing focus on the need to link housing strategy to wider community and corporate strategies and involve a wide range of local stakeholders in identifying needs and planning responses (CIH, 1998), which is in turn linked to:

b) The need to understand housing strategy as an essential element of wider strategies to tackle social exclusion and promote economic, social and environmental well-being. Local authorities are urged to ensure that housing strategy is consistent with and contributes to the achievement of community strategy (DETR, 2001d). New approaches to delivering community strategy and regeneration programmes, such as Local Strategic Partnerships, are intended to strengthen the linkages between housing strategy and other essential service strategies and also with private sector provision. Local authorities will be expected to involve the Local Strategic Partnership in devising housing strategy, alongside other partners and stakeholders (DETR, 2001d).

c) The view that local authorities should develop their community leadership role, and champion the rights of all housing consumers by:
   - facilitating and monitoring the provision of services by other organisations
   - enforcing and promoting high standards of service
   - acting as advocates for community concerns
   - developing citizen participation (LGA, 2000).

d) A new focus on the importance of assessing housing need, demand and supply within the context of the entire housing market, taking account of wider social and economic factors that impact upon the operation of the market.

The approaches that local authorities have traditionally adopted to assess housing need, based on snapshot surveys of a sample of residents, and focussing on the level of unmet demand for (primarily) social housing have generally provided too limited a basis for local housing assessments (CIH/CML, 2000; DETR, 2000c). Local authorities are being encouraged to address private market capacity alongside the functioning of the social housing sector, and to consider both within the wider context of the sustainability of the wider community. An important driver in the focus on housing markets has been the impact of changing demand in some parts of the country, particularly in the Midlands and the North, where some authorities are already actively evaluating demand and supply across tenures (DETR, 2000d). The message is that housing providers can no longer afford to ignore the impact of private sector provision upon demand for public sector homes, or the impact of supply and demand across the entire housing market, even where this extends beyond local authority boundaries.

e)   The Government's commitment to establishing "a stronger strategic role for local authorities" (DETR, 2000a). There is an assumption that separating local authorities' strategic and provider functions will help to strengthen both roles, and authorities are being urged to do this. There are two principal ways in which Government envisaged the split being achieved: through the creation of arms length companies to assume responsibility for the provider role, or through stock transfer. It is unclear whether internal re-organisation to create separate strategic/enabling and provider arms within the organisation would be judged an acceptable degree of separation.

f)   The expectation that local authorities will reflect regional priorities in their housing strategy statements, drawing on and contributing to the regional housing statements that are produced jointly by the Government Offices for the Regions and their respective Housing Corporation Regional Offices, and to work with the new regional agencies that have come into existence since 1999.

Figure 2: Regional Development Agencies and Regional Chambers/Assemblies

In 1999, the Government established a new regional development framework in the shape of nine Regional Development Agencies, each of which has a partner Assembly or Chamber. Whilst in London the Regional Assembly comprises both elected members and a directly elected mayor, elsewhere in England Assemblies (or Chambers) are voluntary groupings of local authority councillors and other private, public and voluntary sector representatives from across each region. Liaison arrangements between the RDAs, Assemblies/Chambers and local authorities are still in the early stages of development, but in the coming years regional strategies are likely to play an increasingly important role in shaping local priorities and plans (and vice-versa).

Whilst the expectation from Government is that the strategic housing role is to be expanded, questions are being asked about the extent to which local authorities are embracing the strategic housing role, and it has been suggested that "many authorities have been distracted from the strategic role by the dominance of the providing role" (LGA, 2000; CIH/LGA, 2001).

It should be noted that even where local authorities have achieved separation between the strategic and provider roles, as is the case in around 100 English local authorities that have carried out large-scale stock transfer, this has not necessarily been accompanied by a strengthening of the strategic housing role in the manner anticipated by Government. Research by Aldbourne Associates in 1997 suggested that stock transfer authorities tended to adopt "one of two approaches". Whilst some authorities had sought to maximise their powers of intervention in the local housing market and to fulfil the potential of the "housing authority function", others had assumed "that stock transfer can be equated with a lessening of housing responsibilities and duties" (Aldbourne Associates, 1997). The same study found that "typically...officers heading up the housing services unit of an enabling housing authority will be third tier officers with very limited staff resources available to them". It is in response to this trend that the LGA has recommended that prior to stock transfer, authorities should be required to produce a business plan specifying how the strategic housing function will be addressed following transfer (LGA, 2000).

This is also one of the factors prompting the CIH and the LGA to call for the introduction of a new statutory strategic housing function (CIH/LGA, 2001). The CIH and LGA have highlighted the fact that there is currently no statutory basis for the strategic housing role, and in particular that:

- there is no statutory requirement to have a housing strategy
- the duty to carry out local housing assessments is too limited in scope, focussing only on the need for additional homes and the physical condition of housing
- there are no express statutory requirements to consult or involve consumers or other agencies (CIH/LGA, 2001).

There is a concern that the strategic role is developing too slowly, and that authorities will not give sufficient priority to the role so long as they are not required to do so by statute (with a threat of financial or legal sanctions for failure to comply). It has been recommended that Government strengthens the law to bring statute in line with best practice, and specifically to:

- require councils to produce regular assessments of the housing market, taking account of housing needs and supply across all tenures
- give local authorities a new duty to prepare, implement and monitor a local housing strategy for their areas, taking account of specific issues
- extend local authorities' powers and duties to intervene in the housing market, including duties to promote choice for consumers, good standards of management in rented housing and the best use of the existing stock
- require councils to consult with neighbouring authorities when assessing housing markets and consider the role that external agencies can play in implementing strategy
- require councils to publish in their local housing strategies their funding priorities, including local authority social housing grant, house renovation grants, and other assistance to private sector residents
- require councils to ensure integration of housing and planning strategies for their areas, to ensure that there is sufficient affordable housing, to promote mixed communities and to enable greater mobility between tenures (IPPR, 2000; CIH/LGA, 2001)

In Scotland and Wales plans are already being considered that would create a statutory basis for the strategic housing role.

In chapter 3 we consider the implications of such a change for English local authorities, and examine whether other measures may also be needed to promote the development of the strategic housing role.

The implications of the new strategic role for RSL/LA relationships

The new demands of the strategic housing role described above have implications for the relationship between RSLs and local authorities, and indeed between RSLs and the Housing Corporation. The presumption is that local authorities will intervene to influence the activities of RSLs as part of the wider strategic agenda, and in particular to:

- Assess the capacity of the RSL sector to meet identified local needs.

- Identify, facilitate and co-ordinate the activities of RSLs to address identified needs.

- Champion the rights of RSL consumers, alongside all other local consumers, and in particular to:
  - promote quality and best practice in the design, provision and management of housing in the area
  - increase consumer consultation and empowerment
  - promote measures to tackle anti-social behaviour and all forms of harassment.

This implies that the relationship between local authorities and RSLs will be developed in ways that extend beyond traditional forms of interaction, to enable local authorities to influence more effectively patterns of provision and standards of service at a local level. This will have implications also for the relationship between local authorities and the Housing Corporation, as it implies that local authorities will have some involvement in areas that have traditionally been the preserve of the Corporation in its capacity as the principal regulator of RSLs.

In chapter 4 we consider the nature of current relationships, and the way in which these need to change to facilitate the development of a new strategic housing role. However, any discussion about relationships between the sectors also needs to consider the implications of the changing profile of the social housing sector.

The changing profile of the social housing sector

Changing patterns of ownership

In recent decades there has been a gradual decline in the relative and actual size of the local authority stock as a consequence of three key factors:

a) *The right to buy.* Since 1979 over 2.26 million council homes have been sold to tenants under the right to buy.

b) *The stock transfer programme.* Since 1988 over 130 English authorities have transferred over 500,000 homes to newly created or existing registered social landlords, representing a major shift in provision from the council to the RSL sector. The Housing Green Paper confirmed the Government's commitment to large-scale stock transfer (alongside the creation of arms-length companies and the Private Finance Initiatives). If the Government continues to support an annual stock transfer programme of 200,000 units a year (the level proposed in the Housing Green Paper and supported in the Spending Review 2000), the RSL sector will own more homes than local authorities by 2005.

c) *New build and acquisition by RSLs*. Since 1988, and changes to the way in which RSL housing is financed, subsidy for new social housing provision has been channelled increasingly through RSLs. New social housing is now provided almost entirely in the RSL sector, with completions of new local authority homes running at less than 500 units per annum nationally since 1997.

For local authorities, the combined effect of these factors is a steady diminution of the size of their stock (Figure 3).

Figure 3: Distribution of stock by tenure (England)

Stock type	1988(1)	2000(2)
Owner-occupiers	66%	68%
Privately-rented	10%	12%
Local authority rented	22%	14%
Registered social landlord rented	3%	6%
Number of dwellings	19.2m	21.0m

(1) *Housing Finance Review 2000/01*, CIH/CML, 2001
(2) DETR Housing statistics postcard (provisional data for 2000)

This pattern of a declining local authority stock is exacerbated in areas of low demand by demolition programmes, where communities are no longer sustainable and housing cannot be brought back into use through regeneration (DETR, 2000d & e).

It is projected that the extent of local authority involvement in housing management will continue to decline. The business planning process for local authority owned housing is likely to highlight this reduction, and assist local authorities in reaching a long-term view of the sustainability of council-owned housing. The Government's expectations concerning the separation of the strategic and provider functions (described above) are linked with the expectation that local authorities will review the viability of retaining a landlord role in the context of Best Value, the "decent homes standard" and the need to maximise stock investment opportunities. It is expected that in many cases, authorities will opt for stock transfer, with council homes moving into the RSL sector.

However, local authorities are encouraged to ensure that stock transfer does not result in the creation of new monopoly suppliers in the social sector. Guidance to local authorities on applying to join the Government's stock transfer programme stresses that authorities should consider the full range of available landlord options, including the transfer of stock to subsidiaries of existing RSLs (DETR, 2000h). This expectation is linked to the wider Government objective of achieving "real variety in the way services are provided and genuine plurality amongst service providers. [The Government] is opposed to any single supplier dominating the provision of services … locally" (DETR, 1999b).

This has particular implications for the shape of the social housing sector; in order to make judgements about the future of council-owned stock, local authorities are expected first to engage with supply markets, to consider their capacity, and to create the conditions in which suitable management and ownership arrangements will be able to thrive in the long term. Decisions about future arrangements for the structure of the social housing sector in any particular council area should not be made in isolation by that local authority, and authorities should seek to preserve diversity and pluralism within the sector. This assumes a level of dialogue with locally operating RSLs that does not exist in many areas.

If current Government programmes are maintained, and local authorities respond to the Government agenda, it is to be expected that the profile of social housing will change radically over the next five years. However there are other factors influencing the shape of the social housing sector.

A wider role for RSLs

The RSL sector is now expected to tackle a much wider range of tasks than in the past. The provision of affordable rented housing still remains the core and majority activity of most developing RSLs. However, the Government's expectations (as described, for example, in the Housing Green Paper) are that RSLs will contribute to meeting a much wider range of needs, and not simply those relating to the traditional social landlord role.

This includes assisting key workers who are required to sustain the local economy, people needing housing with care and support, elderly owner occupiers and (using the terminology of the Green Paper) "well intentioned" private landlords.

The extension of the remit of RSLs has been facilitated by the Housing Corporation's most recent circular on diversity (entitled *Regulating a Diverse Sector* – HC15/00) which considerably loosens the rules on permitted activities and constitutional structures. RSLs are now able to undertake a much wider range of activity within the definition of social housing. The Corporation's overall definition of social housing is "homes for letting or low cost home ownership and associated amenities and services, for people whose personal circumstances make it difficult for them to meet their housing needs in the open market." Specifically, this comprises:

a) housing (included supported housing) covered by the Social Housing Standard

b) short life leasing schemes for homeless families and similar activities which aim to tackle homelessness

c) Private Finance Initiative (PFI) schemes providing they involve the ownership or management of social housing

d) management contracts of publicly owned housing for rent

e) Home Office contracted accommodation for asylum seekers

f) refurbishment or property maintenance companies, provided the bulk of their work is concerned with social housing

g) community regeneration initiatives

h) care and repair contracts (i.e. services for elderly owner occupiers)

i) residential care homes (i.e. registered with social services)

j) domiciliary and social care services (which includes the provision of services to non RSL residents as long as some RSL residents also benefit)

k) shared ownership and other low cost home ownership schemes

l) housing for workers in key public services provided that the rent is below prevailing market rents and the RSL has the power to control the letting, management and termination of the tenancies.

RSLs are permitted (subject to the terms of their constitutions) to undertake even broader functions, subject to restrictions on the use of social housing assets to fund these, and a reporting mechanism. This widening of the RSL remit has important implications for local authority efforts to deliver housing strategy; it is increasingly important to ensure that the activities and resources of RSLs are directed by local authorities to deliver the strategy, both to address the need for social housing and for decent, affordable private sector homes.

However, the broadening of the RSL role has other implications; in particular, it provides an incentive to RSLs to combine to share research and development costs and to absorb the greater risk of abortive costs inherent in projects outside the mainstream. It has been a significant factor in stimulating the creation of group structures and mergers between RSLs.

Group structures and mergers

The last five years has seen the beginning of what are likely to be major changes in the structure of the RSL sector, largely initiated by RSLs themselves. This is a reflection both of the considerable growth of the sector and the widening role of RSLs, described above. In addition, there are other incentives and pressures upon RSLs to increase the quality of their homes and services but at the same time to reduce costs, principally in order to maintain rent affordability. The Government's new rent restructuring system will increase these pressures as rent levels for some RSLs in some areas may need to be reduced and general rent rises will be capped at half a percent, rather than one percent, above inflation. Thus, gaining economies of scale and reducing duplication is an increasingly important issue for RSLs.

For stock transfer RSLs the pressures are even greater. Most are still losing housing stock through right to buy and often cannot develop new homes as fast. Competition from financially stronger, traditional RSLs makes social housing grant harder to secure. A more diverse role potentially allows an RSL to fund its overheads from wider sources of income. Some diverse activities may contribute surpluses to fund other activities or may allow unused or underused assets to be employed.

An increasingly common way of addressing these issues is through the development of a group structure. A group structure exists where one organisation is a subsidiary of another. The definition of a subsidiary is that its membership (i.e. its shareholding or other ownership) and board membership is under the ultimate control of another body (the controlling body commonly being known as "the parent"). A group structure is generally required where an RSL forms other bodies to carry out initiatives. This is because the Housing Corporation expects to see clear constitutional and contractual arrangements between RSLs and bodies that, in effect, work to a common strategy. Group structures can develop when an existing RSL is the parent and new or joining RSLs become subsidiaries. A more common and growing approach is the creation of a completely new parent that is non-asset holding, with a sponsoring RSL becoming a subsidiary of the new parent.

Outright merger of organisations (i.e. two organisations becoming one) is a route that some RSLs have taken. However, for most active and financially healthy RSLs, the idea of merger is unattractive because of the loss of identity and autonomy. Thus, more recently, group structure arrangements have been developed which are geared to the needs of existing and strong organisations that wish to come together.

The following figures chart the changes to the Housing Corporation Register of Social Landlords, which provides an indication of the scale of merger and group structure activity in the sector (Source: Housing Corporation Regulation Division, April 2001):

Figure 4: Transfers of engagement and the creation of group structures

Year	Transfers of Engagement	Creation of Group Structures		
		Creation of parent/ subsidiary relationship	Newly registered subsidiary joins existing group	New non-asset holding parents – creating a new group or reorganising an existing group
1993/94	14	–	–	–
1994/95	25	–	–	2
1995/96	19	7	–	1
1996/97	21	6	2	2
1997/98	21	14	8	7
1998/99	17	19	12	13
1999/00	21	4	10	9
2000/01	11	12	4	11

Virtually all of the restructuring described above has been initiated by RSLs themselves to address corporate business needs. The Housing Corporation has traditionally been reluctant to broker RSL reorganisation other than in "rescue" cases, and in such cases, there is no role for the local authority in brokering or influencing the outcome of merger talks.

However, as noted above, the changing profile of the RSL sector is a matter of increasing importance to strategic housing authorities as they seek to carry out their strategic role. In order to assess the capacity of local housing markets to meet need, and to co-ordinate all available resources to deliver strategy, local authorities have a real interest in whether the RSL sector is capable of delivering. This interest will be of increasing relevance as rent restructuring begins to have an impact. As noted above, restructuring is likely to have an impact upon the viability of some RSLs in some areas, and to result in pressure to merge. In carrying out their strategic housing role, local authorities will want assurances that the sector is capable of responding to the challenge of rent reform, and can continue to deliver an appropriate range of services to meet locally identified needs.

Local authorities also have an interest in the merger debate from the perspective of their role as consumer champion. RSL tenants and leaseholders have a right to be consulted about merger/transfer of engagement proposals, although they have no right of veto, and local authorities might wish to play a part in ensuring that consultation is adequately carried out.

This raises the question of what role, if any, local authorities might play in merger negotiations, a question that we seek to address in chapter 5.

Related to this is the question of the role that local authorities might play in decisions about the rationalisation of RSL management in their areas.

The rationalisation debate

In 1999, there were over 2000 RSLs operating in England, providing over 1.16 million homes (*Key Facts 1999*, Housing Corporation, 2000). Whilst the size of the RSL stock has grown rapidly over the last decade, the number of RSLs has increased only marginally; there were 2,163 housing associations registered with the Housing Corporation in 1989 compared with 2,070 in 1999 (*Key Facts 1999*, Housing Corporation, 2000 and *Housing Associations in 1989*, Housing Corporation, 1990).

The vast majority of RSL stock is owned by a minority of large RSLs.

Figure 5: Distribution of RSL self-contained stock by size of RSL

By size in units	No. of RSLs	% of RSLs	No. of RSL units (000)	% of RSL units
0-250 units	1,689	81%	49.9	4%
251-1000 units	123	6%	64.3	5%
Over 1000 units	264	13%	1164.1	91%
Total	2,076	100%	1278.1	100%

(Source: RSR 2000, Part B, Housing Corporation)

Many RSLs operate in more than one local authority district, some in more than 100:

Figure 6: Number of LA districts in which RSLs with over 250 self-contained (SC) units operate

No. of LAs in which RSLs operate	Number of RSLs	Stock of SC Units	% of SC Stock
1	88	215,842	18%
2 to 10	176	331,255	27%
11 to 21	52	157,450	13%
21 to 40	39	194,143	16%
41 to 60	14	96,802	8%
61 to 100	10	99,501	8%
101 to 200	5	60,501	5%
201+	3	72,828	6%
TOTAL	387	1,228,322	100%

(Source: RSR 2000, Part N, Housing Corporation)

At a local level, the pattern of provision reflects the national picture. In many local authority areas there are large numbers of RSL landlords, relative to the size of the stock, many of which may operate in a number of local authority areas, either concentrated within a particular region, or in some cases across regions.

It has been suggested that some RSLs' stock holdings are too dispersed, and that the scatter of property does not make "sense" in terms of efficient management or meeting local needs. This is particularly the case for communities which are served by multiple landlords, including some consortia estates, where pepper potting of ownership and management may be increasingly difficult to justify under Best Value, and in the context of the neighbourhood regeneration agenda. The suggestion is that in such cases, ownership or management needs to be "rationalised".

However, the term rationalisation has been used to describe a number of different ways (or combinations of ways) of addressing the problem of dispersed stock ownership. These include:

- Achieving a reduction in the number of RSLs operating in any given area.

- Containing RSLs within particular regions (rather than allowing RSLs to operate across any number of regions, as is presently the case).

- Achieving more coherent management arrangements for individual neighbourhoods, whether to address community sustainability or to create more efficient management.

It has been suggested that in some cases rationalisation could be achieved through "stock swaps", with RSLs giving up stock in return for stock elsewhere (CIH, 2000b). This need not necessarily mean a transfer of ownership; it might involve RSLs making local management arrangements so that ownership remains with the original landlord. It has been suggested that the Housing Corporation could facilitate this process by:

- streamlining procedures to allow the transfer of stock between RSLs

- providing funding to support such transfers, and a clearing house to identify and facilitate stock swaps (CIH, 2000b).

Focusing on any particular blue-print for rationalisation, such as limiting the number of RSLs that should operate in any given area, or the geographical extent of their operations, can be problematic. For example, specialist housing providers (such as agencies providing supported housing for particular client groups, and BME providers) may have developed small concentrations of stock across a wide geographical area because this is a cost-effective way of delivering specialist services to small numbers of clients in any given area. It is therefore essential that any debate about rationalisation finds ways of protecting the diversity of the sector where this is important to meet local needs.

Some RSLs are already discussing the rationalisation of management, and have taken steps to transfer the ownership of pockets of property which are better served by other landlords. However, generally the track record of the RSL sector in achieving voluntary stock rationalisation is poor and the pressures on RSLs to consider the need for rationalisation are few. Indeed, for many RSLs the desire to retain a foothold, however small, in areas that might offer future business opportunities, coupled with the negative public relations implications of withdrawing from an area, and asking tenants to consider an alternative landlord, can be strong drivers to retain scattered stock.

The Chief Executive of the Housing Corporation has urged all RSLs to consider the case for change:

> *"Even the biggest associations seem to have a scatter of properties in places which probably don't fit their future corporate needs. At the same time, there are some good smaller associations which are almost anorexic and could do with a square meal of some extra properties to manage close to their core area of operation"* (Chief Executive of the Housing Corporation in speech to the National Housing Federation Chief Executive's Conference, quoted in *Housing Today*, 25 January 2001).

The Corporation has no powers to force RSLs to rationalise management arrangements at a local level, but it has been suggested that it will use its powers of persuasion to encourage RSL boards to consider rationalisation.

Local authorities have no specific powers to influence the shape of the sector, other than through their ability to influence the allocation of social housing grant. Under the current statutory and regulatory framework, the future of RSL operations in any given area is ultimately a matter for RSL boards, and in certain circumstances (such as where the viability of an RSL is in doubt) for the Housing Corporation. Whilst tenants have a right to be consulted, their ability to influence outcomes is limited.

However, it is important to question whether it is appropriate to view the consolidation/rationalisation and merger issue purely as a matter of RSL corporate business. Should any programme of rationalisation/merger also address issues of community sustainability and customer aspirations, and if so, is there a role for the strategic housing authority in facilitating the debate about the shape of the sector? Local authorities should be well placed to help map patterns of provision and to facilitate dialogue about the suitability of local management arrangements, a role that would sit well with their wider strategic responsibilities. However there is at present no express role for them. In chapter 5 we look at the views of case study authorities on the rationalisation/merger issue, and consider what role, if any, there should be for local authorities.

3 The strategic housing role

Introduction

This chapter examines what is involved in delivering the new strategic housing role, focussing specifically on the constraints and difficulties faced by our case study authorities in developing the role. At the end of the chapter we highlight the changes that we think will be needed to enable local housing authorities to develop their approach in the way suggested by Government.

This chapter provides the essential context for our consideration of the relationship between the strategic housing role and the RSL sector in the remaining chapters of the report. It must be emphasised that whilst our brief was to focus on the social housing sector, the strategic housing role must be seen in the round; Government policy is clear in stating that relationships with RSLs should not be viewed in isolation from relationships with the wider range of public and private sector agencies involved in making local housing markets operate effectively.

We look at each of the following issues in turn, drawing on evidence from our case study areas where relevant:

- essential components of the strategic housing role
- issues that local authorities have to address to develop the role, and the constraints that they face
- what changes, if any, are needed to address the constraints identified.

The essential components of the strategic housing role

As has been noted in chapter 2, the statutory basis for the strategic housing function is limited, and there have been calls for the introduction of legislation to give the role added weight. The principal incentive for authorities to develop their strategic role is the fact that the submission of a housing strategy and the ability to demonstrate its effective implementation of strategy are an integral part of the Housing Investment Programme (HIP) assessment process. The DETR has stated that its new approach to HIP appraisal "will have a more strategic focus" (DETR, 2001d). Local authorities will be judged on whether they have:

- accurately assessed housing needs across all tenures
- established clear priorities, with reasons for their selection
- identified effective and efficient strategies, based on an analysis of the range of options available to address priorities
- brought these together into clear action plans, the progress of which can be monitored
- carried out the above processes in consultation with all residents.

Guidance also urges authorities to ensure that the housing strategy development process is linked to the development of the Community Strategy, and that both are be carried out in partnership with the full range of appropriate public and private sector bodies, voluntary organisations and groups. Existing guidance to local authorities provides an indication of the range of stakeholders and agencies that should be involved in strategy development (CIH/LGA, 1998).

In addition, authorities are urged to deliver particular aspects of the strategic role in accordance with new Government guidance on:

- the assessment of need across housing markets (DETR, 2000c), in partnership with other local authorities where relevant
- the assessment of housing stock condition
- the delivery of the full range of enabling functions (see Annex E to draft DETR Guidance on HIP 2001, DETR, 2001d).

The HIP guidance, like much of the guidance that currently exists on the strategic role, is largely about processes or inputs. However, in order to be effective, housing strategy must look beyond process, and address the outcomes that the authority is seeking to achieve. It should also show how the LA will use its enabling (and, if relevant, landlord) functions to contribute to the delivery of these objectives, and describe how the authority will influence those agencies outside the normal remit of the housing enabling function that significantly affect the operation of the housing market and the achievement of the LA's strategic housing objectives.

The objectives of housing strategy should focus on the creation of sustainable housing markets and should be linked to wider corporate and regional strategies for community sustainability, and environmental, social and economic well-being (IPPR, 2000). The IPPR, in its work on the future of social housing proposed a series of overarching objectives for Government housing policy. These goals can equally be translated to the local context, and should be used by local authorities to shape local housing strategies.

For the purposes of this study, and drawing on the IPPR work, we have sought to define what the outcome, or the results, of a successfully performed strategic housing role would look like. In the following tables, we set out:

- figure 7: the range of strategic objectives that could underpin a local housing strategy (local authorities would determine which are appropriate to local circumstances)
- figure 8: the link between strategic objectives and enabling activities, including measures to influence agencies outside the normal remit of the enabling role.

Figure 8 provides an illustration of the range of mechanisms available to assist local authorities to deliver housing strategy; it also seeks to demonstrate how enabling activities should be linked to broader corporate objectives designed to achieve sustainable housing markets.

Figure 7: A housing market that "works well" meets the following strategic objectives

	Strategic objective
A	The market comprises sufficient and accessible housing to meet demand within a defined and reasonable timescale given the nature of the local and regional economy.
B	There is sufficient flexibility to respond to changes in demand within a reasonable timescale and with minimised disruption to communities.
C	There are acceptable short-term solutions (e.g. in the case of homelessness) where the market cannot respond quickly enough to demand
D	Housing stock and the related environment are managed and maintained at a high level so as to:
D1	– combat discrimination and tackle disadvantage
D2	– not create ill health and sustain good health
D3	– maintain a justified sense of safety and security amongst residents and visitors
D4	– make efficient use of resources and maximise use of sustainable resources
D5	– minimise poverty, reduce inequality and tackle the poverty trap
D6	– maximise the opportunity for all the community (including vulnerable people and those with disabilities) to lead a lifestyle of maximum independence
D7	– facilitate strong communities
D8	– create visually attractive places
E	Housing – its condition, appearance and management – contributes to (and at a minimum does not undermine) the popularity of areas.
F	Housing contributes to creating and maintaining a strong local, sub-regional and regional economy, taking account of factors such as employment prospects and access to transport
G	The functioning of the housing market is (as far as is consistent with the other objectives) based on choices made by individual consumers
H	Public intervention through information, advice, support and promotion of good practice can be maximised and funding, regulation and enforcement minimised.

Figure 8: Matrix of strategic and enabling functions required to deliver strategic objectives

No.	Strategic objective	Strategic function	Basis	Enabling
1.	A, B	Assess housing need, demand and supply in all sectors, and the balance within the markets	LA/Sub Reg	• Commission research into operation of housing markets and capacity to meet need and demand across all tenures, in accordance with DETR Guidance • Develop and maintain databases to evaluate need and demand • Draw on existing administrative records (eg housing register, lettings data) to forecast unmet need and demand
2.	D	Assess the quality, condition, and quality of management of the housing stock in the private and social sectors	LA	• Private sector stock condition surveys • Survey of own stock where a landlord • Encouragement of surveys by RSLs • Local benchmarking • Performance monitoring
3.	D4, D5	Assess the energy efficiency of the housing stock in all sectors and promote measures	LA	• HECA surveys • Encouragement of implementation by others
4.	D5, D6, E, F	Identify the contribution to be made by housing and related services, for the achievement of social inclusion and economic well being in the area, and develop and implement strategies	Neighbourhood/ LA/SubReg/ Regional	• Undertake (if landlord) and/or promote neighbourhood management initiatives (single and multi-tenure) • Develop and fund or seek funding for neighbourhood renewal, and contribute to delivery • Include housing related elements in corporate strategies, especially the Community Strategy, and including antipoverty strategy etc. • Corporate liaison • Consultation with businesses and with other agencies influencing and/or involved in addressing social exclusion
5.	A, B, G	Produce strategies for ensuring housing need is met through access to affordable housing	LA/SubReg	• Maintain a housing register • Establish and monitor a lettings scheme • Establish access arrangements with other providers (inc. nominations to RSLs), promoting choice for people in need • Administer and promote take-up of housing benefit

→

No.	Strategic objective	Strategic function	Basis	Enabling
6.	A, B, G	Produce strategies for addressing shortfalls and surpluses in the supply of affordable housing	LA/SubReg/Regional	• Use planning powers to procure affordable and low cost market housing • Provide LASHG and other public funding • Provide free/concessionary land for housing schemes • Use of CPO and clearance powers • Land assembly • Establish/invest in joint venture development bodies (e.g. urban regeneration companies) • Provide serviced sites
7.	A, C	Promote the prevention and reduction of homelessness	LA/SubReg	• Introduce measures to prevent homelessness e.g. furnished lettings, rent deposit, tenancy relations teams • Undertake rough sleeper and other surveys to establish levels and nature • Provide access to advice and support • Assess and determine applications • Provide/procure temporary housing
8.	D	Produce strategies for achieving acceptable stock condition and energy efficiency in the housing market	LA/Subreg	• Administer and award grants for house renovation, group repair, etc. • Establish neighbourhood renewal programmes • Apply CPO powers • Award grants for energy efficiency • Enforce fitness standards, HMO licensing schemes, etc. • Promote HECA measures
9.	D, E, G, H	Intervene to improve the efficiency of the markets	LA/SubReg/Regional	• Procure affordable and low cost housing through planning powers • Provide or facilitate provision of rent deposit guarantee/mortgage guarantee schemes • Use CPO powers to bring empty property into use/change of use • Promote HB takeup • Promote use of HB SLAs to improve liaison with landlords • Promote best practice on mortgage lending amongst local lenders • Apply repair/closure/demolition powers

→

No.	Strategic objective	Strategic function	Basis	Enabling
10.	A	Designate land use for housing in conjunction with planning department and others	LA	• Consult with planning department re: the focus of Local and Structure Plans • Use CPO powers • Initiate surveys
11.	D6	Specifically address the housing and housing related needs of vulnerable people	LA/SubReg/ Regional	• Contribute to development of corporate care strategies, especially Supporting People strategy • Provide revenue and capital funding for housing with care and support • Consult with agencies and other providers • Assess the numbers and needs of vulnerable people requiring housing and related services
12.	D	Promote quality and best practice in the design, provision and management of housing in the area	LA	• Identify the housing design and management needs of specific client groups e.g. disabled people • Promote improved design standards through development agreements and the planning system • Administer grants for aids and adaptations • Introduce landlord accreditation schemes; enforce HMO licensing schemes • Establish/participate in benchmarking clubs and exercises
13.	ALL	Identify, bid for and commit resources to deliver the housing and related strategies	LA/ Subreg/ Regional	• Prioritise needs • Liaison with other funding agencies e.g. Housing Corporation • Fund voluntary agencies to provide advice/support/advocacy • Apply for grant funding from national and EU sources • Allocate funding to RSLs
14.	ALL	Engage other housing providers and relevant agencies in the promotion of housing strategies and provision of housing and related services	LA	• Consult with stakeholders on housing strategy • Promote and develop joint planning and delivery mechanisms • Monitor the performance of RSL and other partners in delivering the strategies
15.	ALL	Promote the interests of residents and local communities, and act as consumer champion in delivery of the strategic objectives	Neighbourhood/ LA/Sub Reg	• Consult with local residents and community representatives • Encourage participation in strategy development processes and forums • Implement Tenants Compact in relation to strategy • Set up cross-tenure consultation structures

STRATEGIC HOUSING ROLE

We turn now to look at the way that case study authorities have responded to some of the key challenges of the developing strategic role:

- the need to develop a cross-tenure focus for housing strategy, and to develop strategy in collaboration with a wide range of stakeholders and residents from all sectors

- the need to develop an understanding of the operation of local housing markets

- the need to set housing strategy within the sub-regional and regional context.

The cross-tenure focus

In Manchester, the City Council has strongly embraced the strategic role, with housing strategy determined by the requirements of a cross-tenure corporate strategy, focussed on the needs of local markets and the intervention required at local neighbourhood level:

Figure 9: Case study example: Manchester City Council and the Strategic Housing Role

The main driver of Manchester's approach to the delivery of its strategic housing function is the need to understand and manage changing demand within local housing markets. The enabling role is geared to the development of a cross-tenure corporate strategy, focussed on the needs of local markets and the intervention required at local neighbourhood level (Corporate Housing Strategy 2001). The City Council has identified the following objectives of housing strategy:

- strengthen the population base, by extending the choice and quality of housing
- attract and retain economically active households, by increasing the supply of higher value homes
- create and maintain housing demand, by intervening in local housing markets and improving physical environments
- build sustainable and healthy communities, by targeting resources to sustain popular areas and create neighbourhoods where people want to live.

In Manchester therefore the balance between the enabling and providing roles within housing strategy is determined by the requirements of local markets. Overall there has been a shift in the allocation of resources towards private sector renewal; in 2001/02 40 per cent of the capital programme will be directed towards the private sector.

Manchester has taken a proactive approach to the involvement and role of the private sector in the regeneration of housing markets and meeting need. The council is clear that its private sector renewal strategy cannot be seen in isolation and the results of its approach are being seen e.g. in the establishment of a cross tenure nuisance team in East Manchester, available to all RSLs, private landlords and residents.

The council also emphasises the need for pro-active planning to ensure that private sector development is directed to complementing local strategy through developments that are appropriate in terms of location, size or type. The council is now actively developing its relationship with house builders so that information on sales can be mapped and trends monitored.

In Brent, considerable focus has been placed on private sector intervention within housing strategy, and the council is beginning to develop cross-tenure approaches on a number of issues, and in particular to tackle anti-social behaviour and fear of crime:

Figure 10: Case study example: The London Borough of Brent and the Strategic Housing Role

Historically, the London Borough of Brent has embraced the enabling role, and measures to intervene in and influence the private sector are a high priority in housing strategy. The principal driver of this has been the high level of housing need in the borough, and in particular the high incidence of homelessness, which has a direct cost for the authority. At the end of 2000, Brent had 3,488 households in temporary accommodation, the second highest figure in London (excluding households accepted as homeless at home (DETR, March 2001).

Additional drivers for the influencing role in Brent are the corporate commitments to tackling social exclusion and inequality, which are reflected through regeneration activities and measures to meet the housing needs of black and minority ethnic communities, and to tackle harassment and discrimination in all sectors. There is a recognition that partnerships with other agencies, including RSLs, are essential to tackle anti-social behaviour and fear of crime, and the authority has put in place cross-tenure initiatives to address these issues.

In 2001/02, 40 per cent of the housing capital programme has been allocated to the private sector, with a further 33 per cent allocated for local authority social housing grant.

In order to develop and implement strategy on a cross tenure basis, authorities need also to ensure that stakeholders from across the tenures are involved in strategy development and implementation. Both Brent and Manchester are beginning to develop their approaches here, with a formal strategy development process that involves a wide range of stakeholders (see the full case study reports published separately). However, neither council has yet engaged representatives of private sector residents in the strategy development process to the extent that local authority tenants have been involved.

Brent Council in particular is hoping to address this gap, and is developing mechanisms for involving residents from the private sector through a regular consultative forum. The intention is to link this forum to the council's decision-making processes, and to secure the more active involvement of private sector residents in future strategy development:

Figure 11: Case study example: The London Borough of Brent and User Consultation

The authority consults users corporately through a variety of mechanisms including a representative citizens' panel, consumer research and consultative forums that operate at local level (Area Forums). There are five Area Forums, which were established in 1997 to provide information about council services to local communities and voluntary organisations, and to give members of the public the chance to express views and concerns about local issues. Meetings are chaired by a ward councillor, and officers reported that they tend to focus on matters other than housing.

The housing service has a separate framework for consulting the communities it serves in both the public and private sectors. In the public sector the principal forums are as follows:

- Area Housing Boards represent council tenants at local level, and enable tenants to be involved in agreeing all capital and revenue-funded major works schemes, reviewing and developing housing management policies, addressing issues such as community safety, anti-social behaviour and community development at area level (with a link to tenants' associations/ community groups operating at estate/neighbourhood level), and monitoring the council's performance against targets.

- Customer panels and contract procurement panels (involving Area Housing Board members) are the means by which the council enables tenants' representatives to take part in the specification, letting and monitoring of housing related contracts.

→

- The Public Sector Management Board. The chairs and vice chairs of each Area Housing Board make up the PSMB, which is the forum through which tenants' representatives are involved in determining HRA investment priorities, rent setting, and providing an oversight of the housing management service. The PSBM is able to refer issues to scrutiny committee, although there is no formal tenant representation on the committee.
- The Leaseholder Forum – a special interest forum that links into the public sector consultation framework.

There are also separate forums to address the interests of council leaseholders, tenant management organisations, and residents of sheltered housing.

The council has been developing its approach to involving private sector residents in recent years. Until recently there were two separate forums for private sector landlords and tenants respectively. These have now been combined to form the Private Housing Forum. The Forum addresses private sector housing strategy and service delivery, and involves shorthold and regulated tenants, tenants living in temporary housing (including RSL managed housing), landlords and home owners. The Forum's relationship with the council's decision-making structures is still being developed, but it has been agreed that the Forum will be able to feed comments through to scrutiny committee and will receive secretariat support in the future.

Locally developed consultation forums have supported area-based regeneration and community development initiatives, across all sectors. These vary in composition and role, depending upon the scope of the project and the wishes of residents. For example, specific consultation/community involvement arrangements exist for Chalkhill and South Kilburn, and to support projects such as the Kilburn Crime Action Zone, a cross-tenure project to tackle crime as a partnership between the housing services in Camden and Brent, the police and local residents and community representatives.

As our case study evaluations illustrate, some local authorities are already developing the strategic role, as a direct response to the demands of local housing markets. In both Brent and Manchester such approaches are seen as essential, although the drivers for this are somewhat different. These approaches have considerable implications for local authorities' relationships with RSLs that are addressed in more detail in chapter 4. Such approaches need also to be underpinned by a better understanding of the operation of local housing markets.

Understanding local housing markets

In order to fully embrace the strategic role, local authorities need to develop approaches to evaluating need, moving away from reliance on the traditional snap-shot surveys that have characterised local authority approaches to assessing need in the past (DETR, 2000c). Whilst periodic surveys have an important role to play, they need to be supplemented by other sources of information to allow projections to be regularly updated, and to support a better understanding of demand and supply at a neighbourhood level. The DETR is also recommending changes to the survey methodologies traditionally used for housing needs surveys (DETR, 2000c).

In its guidance to local authorities, the DETR emphasises the importance of evaluating the operation of local housing markets, and developing data analysis techniques that allow for more robust projections of the scale of unmet need, taking account of the capacity of housing markets to address demand for housing across all price brackets and tenure types. Authorities need to ensure that their assessments address the operation of markets that extend beyond local authority boundaries, as well as understanding what is happening at a neighbourhood level, taking account of all the factors that impact on access to housing in any given community.

The DETR provides examples of the range of questions that authorities should be seeking to answer through local housing assessments:

Figure 12: DETR Guidance on Local Housing Assessments

How much housing (across all tenures and price ranges) is likely to be required in the medium term (10-15 years) and how much of this should be affordable or subsidised (including low cost market)?

How much additional affordable or subsidised housing is required in the short term (3-5 years), with what breakdown in terms of tenure, in which locations and of which type/size?

How much of the requirement can be reflected in targets for affordable housing on large new sites allocated for housing or small rural "exceptions" sites? How much might have to be met through mechanisms to enable access to the existing stock? How much might have to be met outside district boundaries?

How great is the scope to increase the contribution of the existing private sector to meet need, whether through:
- bringing empty properties into use
- providing information and assistance to groups who have difficulty gaining access to, or sustaining, home-ownership or private renting
- working with private landlords to improve standards/secure supply?

How should the budget for local authority stock refurbishment be deployed between different programmes, types of stock and areas?

Should the authority consider stock transfer/private finance/partnership arrangements for any of its housing?

How large a budget should be applied to private sector renewal, and how should it be deployed between priority areas and responsive programmes, and different types of grant support?

Should the authority pursue a rigorous regulatory and enforcement regime in relation to parts of the stock?

What additional specialised housing and support provision will be needed for elderly and disabled people and other groups?

What changes in the eligibility and priority rules and weightings for the allocation of social rented housing may be appropriate?

(DETR, 2000c, Appendix 1)

Housing assessments should not just consider the unmet need for social housing; there should be a wider consideration of all forms of provision (such as for example provision at the low cost end of the market, and key worker housing) and methods to deliver these. Assessments also need to take account of the sustainability of communities, and the impact that new developments and other changes in patterns of provision will have upon the viability of existing communities. In order to develop this understanding, local authorities need to employ a far wider range of tools than they have used in the past.

In Manchester, unlike the other case study areas, housing strategy is already underpinned by research on the operation of local housing markets, and the City Council has developed a database enabling the council and other stakeholders to monitor demand, and the operation of housing markets, on a cross-tenure basis across the city.

Figure 13: Case study example: Manchester City Council and research into local housing markets

The City Council has been analysing and monitoring trends in demand for its own stock for a number of years. Examination of trends in the private sector housing market began in 1996, with the decision to carry out a housing market study in North Manchester. The decision to extend the work on demand analysis to the private sector was prompted by a recognition that markets were declining across all tenures in the area, and the need to understand the implications of this trend for central to plans for regeneration in the city. Manchester has initiated and participated in many studies of demand and the state of housing markets, and has worked with other major cities experiencing similar trends, and with the Centre for Urban and Regional Studies (CURS), to develop an understanding of the factors influencing demand, and to share expertise in addressing the problem.

Building upon the knowledge gained from the CURS research, the authority has since extended its approach to the evaluation of demand, which is now monitored systematically on a city-wide basis. A city-wide Geographical Information System (GIS) was established in 1996, initially drawing on information on council owned stock to monitor demand. Three categories of demand were created based on applicants' waiting times, and the mapping process revealed pockets of low and high demand both by house type and neighbourhood.

From 1997, the system was extended to include demand for RSL property, drawing on a survey of RSLs, and this is currently being updated.

More recently, the system has been extended to allow for the assessment of demand for private sector housing, using market activity reports from the Land Registry and local estate agents.

Housing providers from other tenures can access the system via a web-site, and produce reports/maps, etc, within the terms of a data-sharing agreement.

The GIS is maintained by the council's Housing Demand Team (comprising three officers and reporting to the Assistant Director for Policy and Services). The system has been developed to produce ward profiles, using the toolkit approach developed by John Moores University, which allows the authority to evaluate factors that contribute to the sustainability of each area. Data are collected at the lowest level possible, by property where relevant. Intervention strategies are targeted not just towards areas where the market is collapsing, but also to areas where action is needed to prevent decline.

GIS is also used to map the distribution of house types across the city, to inform aspects of strategy (such as the provision of supported and sheltered housing).

Difficulties in maintaining the system include the use by different statutory agencies of different geographical boundaries, which can make it difficult to evaluate data on a consistent basis (for example, police foot beats do not match ward boundaries, so data on the incidence of crime cannot be readily mapped to other data, and RSL CORE data can only be mapped at postcode level). The council is currently seeking to make better use of council tax data to allow property turnover and void levels to be mapped across tenures.

The GIS is used corporately, as well as by the housing service, for example to map take-up of school places.

Manchester City Council is at the cutting edge in its approach to evaluating the operation of housing markets, with the problems of low demand a key driver. The authority has sought to bring together data on a wide range of social, economic and housing indicators, and disaggregate these at a neighbourhood level, to assist council officers and other agencies in understanding whether communities are failing, and to help plan intervention strategies.

However, Manchester's experience demonstrates the difficulties that local authorities face in seeking to bring together data from a range of sources to support their work on local housing markets. This is a problem that has been recognised by the Social Exclusion Unit through the policy action team dealing with information (Cabinet Office, 2000). The Policy Action Team recommended the development of Neighbourhood Statistics to provide a consistent and comprehensive source of information to support local authorities and others in developing strategies to tackle social exclusion, and addressing related problems such as low demand and unpopular housing. Particular problems identified by the Policy Action Team included lack of consistency in the geographical boundaries used to evaluate data, difficulties specifically in obtaining neighbourhood level assessments of data, and concerns about confidentiality and data sharing.

An internet based information service has recently been established by the Office for National Statistics, and although this is in the early stages of development, the intention is that it will provide a wide range of social and economic aggregate data on a consistent, small-area geography basis, supported by a range of analytical tools. Currently the quality and range of data available generally are very limited, particularly in relation to housing, and work is underway to develop the service in consultation with the agencies that supply and use data, including local authorities (Office for National Statistics, 2000). In the next year the existing datasets are being developed and new datasets added (including improved coverage of housing management and stock condition indicators), and the service is to be publicised and promoted amongst potential users. From 2002 a geographic information service is to be added, and from 2003 census data will be made available through the service at census output area level (20 times more detailed than wards). The service is expected to be fully operational from 2003/04, and will provide local authorities (amongst others) with a ready-made data source, and toolkits for data analysis. This will clearly be of considerable benefit to all organisations involved in strategic planning at a local level, including local housing authorities carrying out the strategic housing role. However, in order to make use of the toolkit and the range of other available data sources on economic and social trends, many local authorities will need to develop their understanding of the role neighbourhood statistics can play in evaluating need and demand, and the wider sustainability of communities.

The other case study authorities are currently reviewing the way that they will respond to the new DETR guidance. It is acknowledged that new approaches will be needed. In the Welland Partnership area, there are plans to commission research into local housing markets across the sub-region, with partner authorities working together to fund and carry out the evaluation.

Figure 14: Case study example: The Welland Partnership and research into local housing markets

> The Housing Group within the Welland Partnership has identified the need to address the operation of local housing markets across the sub-region, because housing supply and demand within individual district and county boundaries appear to be influenced by activity across the wider sub-region. Particular areas to be addressed include the impact of travel to work issues on demand, and the degree of interaction between rural and urban communities. The Partnership plans to commission research into the issue in collaboration with registered social landlords. Each of the partner authorities has independently commissioned housing needs research over the past five years, and it was not felt to be appropriate at this time to conduct a further, joint examination of housing need.
>
> →

It is anticipated that the information provided through the study will assist in the development of Partnership strategy, and will underpin a range of strategic initiatives. The decision of Partnership authorities to work together on this issue also enables them to benefit from economies of scale, an important consideration for smaller districts and unitary authorities. The authorities have previously conducted joint research into tenant aspirations to achieve economies of scale; in this case, there was no particular need to provide a sub-regional overview, and survey data have been evaluated on an individual authority basis. However, the joint approach enabled the Partners to pool resources, share expertise and generate information in a common manner (to facilitate benchmarking).

It was felt that the development and use of Geographic Information Systems is also viable for small authorities where development is viewed as a corporate responsibility and costs are shared. One of the Partnership authorities, Harborough, uses GIS to support its choice-based lettings scheme, and noted that the system is widely used throughout the authority and supports strategy development across a range of functions.

All authorities need to develop an awareness of the way that changes in patterns of provision in neighbouring areas impact upon need and demand. In the Welland Partnership area, joint working across borders is seen as essential to develop the partners' understanding of the operation of the housing market and to support the development of the Partnership's strategic role. Such an approach is likely to be of relevance to other authorities also, not just in rural areas, but also in other regions where administrative boundaries do not fit with the operation of local housing markets.

Working with neighbouring authorities and regional agencies

A particular challenge for local authorities is the need to increase collaboration with neighbouring authorities and regional agencies. This is important to deliver the Government's wider agenda to provide a regional dimension in economic and community regeneration, and to ensure that local strategic plans are consistent with broader regional objectives. Recent research by the LGA suggests that in many parts of the country there is a considerable amount of work to be done simply to raise the profile of the regional agenda, and increase understanding of the role of regional agencies (LGA, 2001).

The case study areas illustrate the range of ways in which some local authorities are developing cross-border working, and are beginning to embrace the regional and sub-regional dimension through partnership working (see figure 15 opposite).

As has been noted above, the Welland Partnership is a well-established alliance of local authorities with similar characteristics forming a sub-region within the East Midlands. The Partnership has carried out a range of initiatives to enable council tenants to access services at any local authority service point across the Partnership area and has plans to develop a strategic approach at sub-regional level. However, whilst the very existence of the Partnership and its achievements to date demonstrate the benefits, the Partnership itself has some difficult issues to address in terms of its links with other partners (see figure 16).

Figure 15: Case study example: The London Borough of Brent and Sub-Regional/Cross Border Partnerships

Sub-Regional Partnerships

Brent is a member of the West London Alliance alongside the London Boroughs of Ealing, Hammersmith & Fulham, Harrow, Hillingdon and Hounslow. The alliance was developed to pursue opportunities for joint working where these address common needs, both by sharing best practice and exploring the scope for joint bidding/joint commissioning and partnership working. One of the motivating factors for the alliance was an attempt to respond to the perceived flow of resources to east London boroughs, which score more highly in deprivation indices, by raising the profile of the area to attract resources. There is also an element of seeking to exploit economies of scale where joint working is appropriate. The alliance operates at both member and senior officer level, and is supported by a range of sub-groups focusing on particular strategic issues/areas. Housing services have a well-established alliance forum at director level. There is a recognition of the need to address housing markets and housing strategy at the sub-regional level, and this is reflected in the existence of liaison/joint working on issues such as homelessness, opportunities for joint development of new housing and joint approaches to supported housing provision (and supporting people), increasing consumer choice and flexibility in letting social housing and the provision of housing in a range of tenures for key workers.

Examples of joint working include the submission of a joint bid for a flexible lettings scheme, also in partnership with RSLs, which has now been selected as one of the choice-based pilot projects by the DETR.

Alliance partners recognise that on some issues, sub-alliances may be required (for example on issues affecting cross-border working for just some of its member organisations). For Brent this has meant partnerships with Ealing and Hammersmith & Fulham on initiatives such as "Refugees into Jobs" where the boroughs share a problem that is not common to the wider alliance, or for example to address cross-border regeneration initiatives such as the Park Royal regeneration programme.

Brent does not view the West London Alliance as its sole sub-regional partnership. Indeed, in terms of socio-economic profile, Brent probably has more in common with its eastern/inner London neighbours, and the borough is fringed by four authorities which are not part of the West-London Alliance (Kensington & Chelsea, Westminster, Camden and Barnet). The authority has therefore maintained partnerships with other neighbouring authorities.

Regional issues

Regional government for and government-led investment in London is now provided through a number of statutory agencies and quasi-government bodies, as follows:

- Greater London Authority, established in 2000 to provide an elected regional assembly for London. Responsibilities include planning, transport and policing. The GLA does not have a housing brief, although it is responsible for formulating London's Spatial Development Plan, which provides the policy context for individual council's Unitary Development Plans. The GLA has also been vocal in championing the need for affordable housing in London and in promoting debate about how best to meet need (see for example, *Homes for a World City*, GLA, 2000).
- London Development Agency, also established in 2000 following the set up of the GLA. Responsible for co-ordinating regional economic development and regeneration.
- Government Office for London.
- Housing Corporation Regional Office.
- The Association for London Government, representing all London authorities (which provides a regular forum for liaison with RSL representatives through the London Housing Federation).

Given that the GLA and the LDA are still in the early stages of development, relationships between the housing service and these organisations have still not been clearly defined. Links between Brent's planning service and the GLA will therefore need development. As far as the housing service is concerned, current liaison is focusing on understanding how the GLA is operating, and what its input on housing issues is likely to be.

The LDA have established a clear agenda for addressing the linkages between economic regeneration and wider regeneration activities. The organisation is currently consulting on how best to involve local authorities and others in forming regional development strategies. Brent sees its role as raising the profile of the area within regional plans, promoting the needs of the community and bringing agencies together where relevant.

The authority has well-established relationships with GOL, the Housing Corporation and the ALG. The authority is currently developing a joint-commissioning approach to the procurement of RSL homes, which is being developed in partnership with the Housing Corporation.

Figure 16: Case study example: The Welland Partnership and County/Regional links

The regional dimension
The Partnership is also still in the early stages of developing its relationships with external partners at a regional level. Key agencies are the Housing Corporation, the Government Office for the East Midlands and the Regional Development Agency and Assembly. The Partnership presents an administrative "complication" in that it does not sit neatly within the existing sub-regions used by regional agencies, which are:

- North Notts and Derbyshire Coalfields
- Southern (incorporating East Northants and Harborough)
- Peak
- Three Cities
- Eastern (incorporating South Kesteven, Rutland and Melton).

Welland Partnership authorities (and the RSLs interviewed for the study) are convinced of the relevance of the Welland sub-region, and are keen to see regional partners adapt to accommodate the group. This has particular implications for grant allocations, for example through the Housing Corporation's approved development programme, which are discussed further below.

Officers commented that the regional development agency and assembly are providing a strong lead in establishing a framework for sustainable development in the region, and the Partnership wishes to play a part in driving that agenda and establishing a place for the Welland sub-region (possibly as a local strategic partnership). One of the officers interviewed sits on the Regional Assembly's social exclusion task group and reported considerable interest in establishing sub-regional partnerships as a vehicle for regeneration. There is a view that the regional dimension will be an increasingly important influence in shaping strategy, displacing to a certain extent the influence of the counties. There is still much work to do in defining the inter-relationship between regional agencies and the two tiers of local government.

Relationships with County Councils/Health Authorities/the Police
Officers noted that a common characteristic amongst partner authorities was a sense of distance from their respective counties; the sub-regional boundary makes more sense in many aspects of strategic planning.

Relationships between the Partnership and the three county council partners and health and police authorities have not been formalised to date. There is a significant practical problem in that the partnership area covers three counties (in addition to Rutland County). Officers advised us that until now housing initiatives have focussed on service areas with no significant implications at county level. Individual authorities have maintained relations at county level as appropriate.

However, in order to move housing strategy forward this will need to change. The Partnership is keen to develop joint working on commissioning supported housing projects, and also to develop a more strategic approach to the management of the planning process, issues which will need to involve close working with social services, health authorities and planning partners. Officers reported that there has been a strong interest from Leicestershire's police authority (which also covers Rutland) in the development of cross-border initiatives, but that work in this field has yet to be developed on a Partnership basis (initiatives exist at authority level).

Officers believe that the process of managing the county dimension may be difficult in cross-boundary schemes. However, officers hope that as the sub-regional identity of the partnership is strengthened it will be possible to begin to develop responses that will enable joint working across administrative boundaries.

The Welland Partnership experience also suggests that authorities considering the formation of alliances and cross-border partnerships need to consult fully on the implications of such arrangements, particularly at regional level, to ensure that they have both an internal and external coherence.

Issues and constraints to be addressed

In addition to the challenges that local authorities face in delivering the broader definition of the strategic housing role, the case studies suggest that there are two specific constraints to be addressed if all authorities are to develop their approach:

- the implications of separating the strategic and provider roles
- the way the new strategic role will be resourced.

Separating the strategic and provider roles

As noted in chapter 2, a key element of the Government's proposals for the strategic housing role is the expectation that there will be an organisational separation between the strategic and provider functions. The Government proposes that this is achieved through the creation of arms length companies, or through stock transfer. We examined the ways in which case study organisations are responding to this aspect of policy.

In both Manchester and Brent, the strategic and landlord roles have been separated within the housing directorate, and both authorities are currently undertaking options appraisals that will determine whether there should be any further separation of roles, either through the creation of arms length companies and/or further transfers of council housing.

In Manchester, the council "is considering the early separation of its strategic and housing management functions" (2000 HIP Operational Information, Manchester City Council). There has been some informal discussion about how the authority would resource the strategic role following transfer of the provider role to independent, or arms-length, companies.

In Brent both officers and the member interviewed for the study expressed concern about the implications of a complete separation between strategic and provider roles, because of the impact that such a split might have on the authority's capacity to sustain an effective strategic role. Concerns focussed on the de-skilling of the service, and a reduction in the authority's ability to think strategically. Members have expressed concern about the impact of LSVT on the authority's power to procure affordable housing to meet need, related to a concern that the levers of influence on the RSL sector are insufficient.

There has been no formal consideration of the need to separate the strategic and provider roles within the Welland Partnership, a reflection of the fact that the roles are integrated within most of the partner authorities. Partnership officers view the provider role as a core element of the strategic housing role. One of the Welland Partners, East Northamptonshire District Council, is currently in the process of transferring its stock to a newly created RSL, East Northamptonshire Housing (within the Longhurst Housing Group). However, the Partnership's housing group is considering involving a representative of the new RSL to join the group, an indication of the importance of the provider role within Partnership strategy.

Partnership members also questioned the feasibility of achieving a separation of the strategic and enabling functions in small local authorities. Rutland County Council, the smallest Partnership member, illustrates their concerns. Rutland is committed to maintaining a strategic housing role, but the extent of enabling activity carried out by the authority is limited. Further, because of the small size of the establishment, it is not felt to be viable to maintain separate teams to carry out the strategic/enabling and provider roles. The administration of private sector grants is delivered from within the Technical Services Team, which delivers services to the public sector, whilst the management of RSL development and corporate liaison rests with the head of service (who also has overall responsibility for the provider role). Similarly, responsibility for managing homelessness and the housing register rests with the tenant services team.

Officers' view is that without a provider function (for example, following stock transfer), the authority could not sustain an effective strategic/enabling role. From Rutland's perspective, a more developed form of the Welland Partnership would offer a possible location for the function.

This raises the question of whether local authorities, and particularly the smaller district councils, are the most appropriate location for the strategic function when it is provided in isolation from the landlord role. There are a number of reasons why, in such cases, it may be preferable to move the role elsewhere. These include:

- Many strategic housing issues cross LA boundaries.
- People do not regard LA boundaries as defining the scope of their lives whether for living, working or accessing other services.
- Important housing functions (e.g. the allocation of funds by the Housing Corporation) do not operate at LA level.
- Being located within an LA does not necessarily mean that a wide range of services can be easily co-ordinated; the majority of housing authorities are district councils, with counties running services that are highly relevant to the strategic housing role.

In some areas, or for small authorities, these arguments may be persuasive. However, there are also many advantages in keeping the strategic role with local authorities:

- Moving the strategic housing role away from LA level is likely to dilute accountability.
- Moving it to regional or sub-regional level will make sensitivity to neighbourhood and community needs even more difficult to achieve.
- The existing LA structure allows the strategic housing role to have a strong neighbourhood and community input and many LAs are using new forms of political organisation to strengthen community and neighbourhood planning.
- The housing role of LAs is recognised – even if the breadth is not fully appreciated – by the public, and any change would cause confusion.
- Even though not all housing authorities are unitaries, they run a range of functions (including local planning) that are highly relevant to the strategic housing function.

There is, in our view, no single ideal location. Some strategic housing issues will be regional, others sub-regional and some highly localised. Given this, there is a strong case for leaving the strategic function with local authorities even after stock transfer. However, in order to address the constraints faced by smaller authorities, it may be appropriate to give local authorities the power to relocate or delegate the function, or aspects of the enabling role, following stock transfer. Options include:

- Local authorities could be given the power to delegate any statutory function to an external agency (including ones formed as joint ventures with partners) in order to facilitate social and economic regeneration. A scheme of delegation would need to be approved by DETR (and any other relevant Government department), which, inter alia, would need to include methods of accountability and performance targets.

- Local authorities that have transferred their housing stock should be permitted to create a strategic housing service with neighbouring LAs; DETR should provide funding for a pilot programme.

As noted above, the case for a transfer of the function in some cases is partly influenced by cost, and the impact of the loss of cross-subsidy from the housing revenue account (and council tenants' rents) to support the strategic role following stock transfer. Whilst this is most keenly felt in small authorities, all local authorities will face increased costs in developing the strategic role, whether or not stock transfer is involved.

Resourcing the role

There is a need to examine further the resourcing of the strategic housing function. Responsibilities, such as that of 'consumer champion', will have organisational implications that need to be addressed. In the following chapter we discuss the particular implications of new definitions of the role for local authority relationships with RSLs. Again, there will be a cost.

For authorities that have not traditionally intervened extensively in the private sector, new definitions of the role will have a particular financial implication. However, for all authorities, large or small, there is a cost to be addressed. As noted above these costs are likely to be more keenly felt in small authorities where a separation of the provider and strategic functions would leave only a skeleton establishment to deliver the strategic role.

There may be a need to review revenue support grant provision to local authorities, to reflect the new demands of the strategic housing role. Any review of RSG provision should in our view be linked to a clear statement of the role itself, and the outcomes that Government expects local authorities to achieve (such as that suggested above). This could also take account of whether or not local authorities have transferred their stock, and are allowed to play an increased role in overseeing the allocation and monitoring of development funds to RSLs (see chapter 4).

The case for a statutory role

Recent research by the LGA suggests that some local authorities are still failing to acknowledge the breadth of new definitions of the strategic role, and that whilst many more do understand its breadth and importance, they have yet to translate this into effective action (LGA, 2001). There is a strong case for addressing the resource implications of the new strategic role alongside the creation of a new statutory duty, as recommended by the CIH, LGA and the IPPR. This would give considerable weight to Government policy, providing both carrot and stick to encourage the development of the role.

The LGA and CIH have produced a series of recommendations on the nature of the obligations that should be enforceable through statute. We recommend that these requirements are extended, as follows, and are accompanied by new obligations for RSLs and Regional Development Agencies:

Figure 17: Developing a statutory strategic function

CIH/LGA Recommendation	Supplementary requirements
Require councils to produce regular assessments of the housing market, taking account of housing needs and supply across all tenures	The duty should include a requirement to identify (in collaboration with other LAs and RDAs) housing markets that cross LA boundaries including sub-regional and regional markets (see complementary requirements for RDAs below). The statutory planning framework should require the LA (as planning authority) to assess the effect on land use designation on the existing housing market and to seek the views of the relevant (including neighbouring) housing authorities and social landlords.
Give local authorities a new duty to prepare, implement and monitor a local housing strategy for their areas, taking account of specific issues	The housing strategy should have clear targets and LAs should be required to publish performance reports (say) every three years on progress towards their achievement. Given the significant and increasing role that RSLs are playing in delivering LA strategies, LAs should be required (say) every 3-5 years to prepare an RSL sector "Expectations Statement" – detailing what is needed from the sector – and locally operating RSLs should produce a "Capacity Statement" identifying what the sector can deliver locally and how any gaps can be filled. The Housing Corporation should provide funding for this process and act as "auditor" of the Capacity Statement. LAs should be encouraged to undertake this exercise jointly with other LAs
Extend local authorities' powers and duties to intervene in the housing market, including duties to promote choice for consumers, good standards of management in rented housing and the best use of the existing stock	Where conventional private sector guidance and enforcement is not judged by an LA to be effective, LAs should be able to support or participate in the creation of joint venture bodies with RSLs and others to improve standards and reshape supply within the private owner occupied and rented sector. The use of SHG (both LA and HC) should be widened to include the funding of these vehicles where the outputs will be housing either affordable to people unable to access housing on the open market or accessible to current social housing tenants. Where these bodies require funding, authorities should be encouraged to use a range of funding methods appropriate to the business, including equity investment and loans.
Require councils to consult with neighbouring authorities when assessing housing markets and consider the role that external agencies can play in implementing strategy	RDAs and (in two-tier local government areas) counties should be under a statutory duty to collaborate with housing authorities in the preparation of housing strategies and the conduct of needs assessments. RDAs should contribute to funding and jointly commissioning the necessary studies. The monitoring of RDA (and county council) performance should include this activity.

As noted above, the creation of a statutory strategic function could be accompanied by arrangements allowing authorities that have transferred their housing stock to establish alternative arrangements for the delivery of the strategic role.

4 The relationship between local authorities and RSLs

The changing national context

The new demands of the strategic housing role have wide-ranging implications for the relationship between local authorities and RSLs. Just as local authorities are expected to intervene more extensively to evaluate and influence local housing markets, so there is an expectation that authorities will intervene to influence the capacity and operation of the RSL sector. In particular, authorities will need to consider how they:

a) exercise their role as consumer champion in relation to RSLs and their tenants

b) promote best practice and the adoption of Best Value amongst all social housing providers (including arms-length providers and any residual local authority provision)

c) address the neighbourhood renewal agenda in partnership with RSLs, including through the formation of local strategic partnerships that involve locally operating RSLs

d) encourage RSLs to consult and empower their residents

e) address the Government's agenda for increasing choice for consumers

f) influence the capacity and co-ordinate the activities of RSLs to meet identified needs.

At present the Housing Corporation is itself responsible for ensuring that RSLs achieve appropriate performance standards and consult and involve their residents. The implication of Government policy is that local authorities will start to play a part in each of these areas, requiring a re-appraisal of the respective roles of and relationship between local authorities and the Corporation. Indeed, the Government has suggested that the local authority role might be extended further, to address the allocation of investment funds. It has been suggested that where local authorities "are no longer directly responsible for the management of the social housing stock", there could be "an increased role in the Corporation's decisions on scheme selection and allocations and in monitoring the performance of RSLs in their area" (DETR, 2000a).

This mirrors plans that are being developed in Scotland, where the Scottish Executive has agreed that local authorities transferring the whole of their housing stock to RSLs may take on from Scottish Homes responsibility for allocating development funding in their area. These plans are part of a broader initiative to develop a more strategic role for local authorities, which includes a statutory requirement on councils to produce a local housing strategy for their area that replaces the separate plans previously produced by Scottish Homes and individual authorities. In cases where council housing has been transferred, local authorities will take on direct responsibility for the local housing budget, which will be the primary source of development funding. Whilst it is intended that there should be a link between stock transfer and greater control of development funding, the executive has not ruled out allowing other councils greater responsibility for allocations where RSLs, funders and other stakeholders support this.

The explicit link between a greater influence and the removal of the provider role should be noted here. The inference is that where local authorities continue to be landlords, there is a potential for conflict of interest undermining the strategic role. Some RSLs interviewed for the study suggested that there may be a potential for conflict of interest where local authorities with a landlord function (and a potential interest in stock transfer) seek greater influence over the RSL.

Government policy suggests that major changes are needed to the strategic housing role. However, at present there is no clear remit for local authorities in carrying out any of the tasks identified above; the regulation and inspection of the RSL sector, and the allocation of investment funds are the preserve of the Housing Corporation. Any development of the strategic function in the manner described above will need to be accompanied by a clearer definition of the relationship between local authorities, the Housing Corporation and RSLs. If, as the DETR has suggested, local authorities take on more responsibilities in relation to RSL funding and regulation, this will be essential.

Case study experiences

We examined the nature of these relationships during our case study visits. Case study authorities employ a number of mechanisms to influence RSL performance, as follows:

- allocating social housing grant (including joint commissioning)
- promoting best practice
- liaison and consultation
- arrangements for the LSVT RSL sector.

We look below at each of these mechanisms in turn.

Allocating social housing grant

Historically, the process of allocating social housing grant (both for the provision of new social housing units and for initiatives to bring private sector properties into use) has been the focus of local authority activities to evaluate and monitor RSL performance, with the emphasis placed upon evaluating the capacity of RSLs that are seeking to develop a scheme, and monitoring the performance of RSLs that are in receipt of grant. The extent of the evaluation and monitoring undertaken by local authorities varies; whilst for some local authorities the overall performance of an RSL is taken into account when grant is allocated, for others the principal concern is the value for money offered by RSLs in terms of unit numbers, access to nominations and rent levels.

Local authorities adopt a range of approaches to allocating funds for development/ regeneration, within the policy framework established jointly by local authorities and the Housing Corporation through regional investment statements.

These include the following:

a) Development partners can be selected on a scheme by scheme basis, possibly through competition, based on criteria established by the authority which frequently address issues such as design and development standards, nominations, rent levels and tenure mix.

b) The authority might select a number of preferred partners, who then bid to deliver schemes based on criteria established by the local authority. The process of selecting preferred partners may involve an analysis of a wider range of criteria than is the case where partners are selected on a scheme by scheme basis. In some authorities preferred partners operate in geographical zones.

c) The authority might select preferred partners in consultation with the Housing Corporation through a joint commissioning process, with the expectation of a longer-term relationship (see figure 18 for a description of joint commissioning). This might include "zoning" of areas of operation for each preferred partner or group of partners.

Both Brent and Manchester are preparing to introduce or have introduced joint commissioning of RSLs to deliver a portion of the approved development programme. The details of each authority's approaches are set out in the case study examples below. Figure 18 provides a description of what joint commissioning entails, and the Housing Corporation's plans for its extension:

Figure 18: Joint commissioning

Joint commissioning is a process for allocating social housing grant involving collaboration between the Housing Corporation, one or more local authorities and other stakeholders. The process involves schemes that span a number of years, so that the annual bidding process becomes less relevant.

To date the Housing Corporation has entered into joint commissioning arrangements with around 80 local authorities.

In its consultation paper *Developing the new approach to investment* (Feb 2001) the Corporation announces its intention to develop and extend joint commissioning, alongside plans to introduce a two stage bidding process, allow for submission of bids through the year, and to develop a three year allocation pool. This proposal complements the Corporation's decision to move away from the distribution of resources using the HNI to a more strategic approach, reflecting regional and sub-regional priorities (as defined through Regional Housing Statements and Housing Corporation Regional Investment Strategies).

Joint commissioning is to be developed for use to commission schemes that meet key regional investment priorities, allowing for programmes with a cross-border dimension or indeed with a specific "needs" focus within a local authority area. Schemes are likely to include:
• supported housing
• rural housing
• regeneration initiatives
• initiatives to address needs in areas of economic/population growth.

A good practice guide is to be published in 2001, building on early experiences.

Joint commissioning is resource intensive, and unlikely to be suitable for LAs with small development programmes (although it reduces the costs associated with competitive bidding). The Corporation says it could not resource it on a universal basis.

Until this year, both Brent and Manchester had accepted bids from RSLs on an open competition basis. Both authorities have active stock transfer/regeneration programmes, and have used separate arrangements for the selection of partners to deliver these programmes.

In Brent, joint commissioning has been introduced in part to avoid the need for repeated evaluation of RSLs through open competition, and therefore to allow for better use of council resources in dealing with RSLs. The council also hopes to be able to enhance the contribution made by partner RSLs to meeting strategic objectives, and is specifically seeking RSLs with the capacity to work across borough boundaries. The authority has no agenda for the rationalisation of housing management or ownership, other than to the extent that partner RSLs will be the primary providers of new housing over the three year period of the partnership. The authority has no plans for "zoning" partners' activities, and will reserve a portion of ADP for allocation outside the joint commissioning framework to allow for the continued involvement of other agencies. Brent Council is strongly committed to the promotion of BME RSLs; it aims to ensure that a minimum of 20 per cent of new units are transferred to BME RSLs (for management or ownership) each year (Brent RSL Development Strategy 2000-2003). It also promotes the transfer of additional units to small specialist BME RSLs and unregistered housing associations. These targets will be retained within the joint commissioning process.

In Brent, therefore, diversity is built into the system.

Figure 19: Case study example: The London Borough of Brent and Joint Commissioning

The council is seeking around 6 strategic partners (who will be invited to play a part in the LSP) who can meet a range of criteria concerning management, development and organisational performance. Joint commissioning will be used to allocate up to 75 per cent of allocations for general needs and shared ownership housing. The remaining portion will be allocated on a scheme-by-scheme basis, and used to promote initiatives such as the commitment to support BME RSLs. Separate commissioning arrangements will apply to the selection of partners for regeneration initiatives, the provision of temporary accommodation and supported housing.

The council will continue to support BME RSLs, but is not being prescriptive about whether the larger BME RSLs apply for preferred partner status or seek to operate as partners to developing RSLs.

Selection Criteria
The council has identified ten criteria against which initial applications from RSLs will be short-listed:
- Demonstration of financial health, strength and innovation.
- Demonstration of in-depth and high quality management resources (organisational strength).
- Development performance: track record of achieving targets on time within budgets; commitment to developing high quality homes that people want to live in; experience of innovative funding approaches; demonstration of Egan compliance and partnering practices; experience of s106 schemes and constructive working with planners and developers.
- Demonstration of effective and responsive housing management performance, including proximity of local management base, track record of performance against key PIs (arrears, void turnaround, etc).
- Asset management strategy and commitment to maintain quality accommodation in Brent.
- Experience of contribution to local and regeneration strategies that enhance residents' quality of life.
- Demonstration of promoting active tenant participation in the provision and management of social housing.
- Demonstration of positive partnership working (developers, BME RSLs, cross-borough working).
- Commitment to Best Value principles.
- Experience of community development and social exclusion initiatives, including people with disabilities.

→

The above criteria are underpinned by a number of essential requirements reflecting both corporate policy and Housing Corporation requirements, which are:
- Demonstration of local presence.
- Adherence to existing and planned Brent protocols.
- Contribution to Brent Housing Group and its sub-groups.
- Input to relevant forums (e.g. strategic partnership group, racial harassment working group).
- Adherence to Housing Corporation Performance Standards.
- Submission of timely and accurate performance information.
- Attendance at performance monitoring meetings.
- Provision of a designated link officer.

In addition, there are a number of specific housing management, development and financial requirements (LBB Joint Commissioning Update, Feb 2001).

The selection panel will involve representatives of a range of stakeholders, as follows:
3 Elected Members; 3 Housing Officers; 1 Housing Corporation Officer; 1 Planning Officer; 1 Tenant Representative.

Committee papers highlight the council's objective of achieving an effective partnership with the Housing Corporation. The council has been explicit in stating that the joint commissioning process is not intended to duplicate the Corporation's regulatory role. Instead, the council expects that information available to the Housing Corporation through its regulatory role will be utilised both when partners are selected, and to monitor their performance. RSLs will be asked to sign up to a partnership agreement (not legally binding). Continued involvement as a partner will be subject to performance review. An issue for the authority is how to minimise the burden of performance monitoring for RSLs. The authority is aware that RSLs are under pressure to provide information in a variety of forms for a number of audiences (including different councils). Officers see a need for joint working, possibly through the ALG and with the LHF/Housing Corporation, to develop a model framework. This should build upon the information that RSLs are already expected to record.

In Manchester the aim of the council's joint commissioning proposals is to achieve "a more coherent management of place by RSLs working in long term partnerships with the City Council and the Housing Corporation" and the vision encompasses:
- rationalisation of stock ownership and/or management
- a reduction in the large number of RSLs operating in the city
- identification of lead RSLs who will actively develop and deliver regeneration proposals for their areas.

In this sense the joint commissioning proposals go much further than the delivery of future housing and housing related projects, and embody an explicit and public strategic vision about the future shape of the RSL sector in the city:

Figure 20: Case study example: Manchester City Council and Joint Commissioning

Joint commissioning is being piloted in three areas within the city. The intention in the pilot areas was to select three to four preferred RSL partners of whom one would be the "lead partner". The council will indicate its intentions on the selection of the lead partner although this could effectively rotate between the preferred partners. The lead partner will be expected to represent the views of the other preferred partners and other RSLs operating in the area, and co-ordinate activity including ensuring RSL contributions to the area; proposals for development activity; action to achieve improved management performance; pursuance of stock rationalisation.

Selection Process
Selection criteria were designed in consultation with the Housing Association Forum and set for each for the three areas, and weighted to reflect the particular needs of the area. In addition the financial capacity and development performance of bidding RSLs were assessed using information supplied by the Housing Corporation from its regulatory function. →

The criteria for the pilot areas were designed to enable assessment based on RSL performance in respect of:
• strategy and Best Value
• partnership and regeneration
• service delivery
• tenant participation.

Information was gathered by means of a questionnaire to bidding RSLs, containing 34 questions based around each of these criteria:

Strategy and Best Value covered such issues as business plans and their relationship to the council's corporate housing and local strategies; views on the priorities for the investment in the pilot areas and plans for growth, stock investment and rationalisation of activity. They also included questions on the RSL's plans for housing service review; review of procurement strategies in the light of Best Value; benchmarking arrangements; and involvement of residents in the planning and delivery of housing services.

Partnership and regeneration questions covered how RSL business and development plans had been influenced by customer consultation; the nature and scope of work with private sector developers and private sector landlords; stock transfer activity; activity to promote diversification of tenure; and action on non-housing activity including community safety, employment, education, health together with the nature and scope of joint working arrangements with other agencies to achieve objectives.

Service delivery evaluation included an examination of all service delivery functions and the extent to which they were delivered locally, including policy and practice on crime and antisocial behaviour; the setting of standards and targets and the involvement of residents in this process; accessibility of services to disadvantaged groups; void management; membership of the Manchester Common Housing Register; local lettings policies and performance and complaints monitoring procedures.

Tenant Participation involved assessment of the bidding RSLs' policies and objectives; how the policy had been developed and the involvement of tenants in its development; involvement of tenants in decision making processes on a range of service delivery issues; their involvement in budget setting, rents, repair and improvement and the business plan; the nature and type of support given to tenants' associations; feedback from satisfaction surveys and how monitoring and review of tenant participation policies was undertaken.

Responses to each question were given a score out of 5 and the scores aggregated for each of the categories. Weightings were then applied for each category to give a total for each submission. The weighting given to each of the four criteria was varied to reflect its significance in each area. In particular the northern quarter required a stronger emphasis on the ability of the RSLs bidding for preferred partner status to deliver strong partnerships because of the burgeoning market and competition for property in the area.

The proposals for joint commissioning have been developed in consultation with the Housing Association Forum. Manchester Housing and the Housing Corporation jointly carried out evaluation. The decision making process was open and transparent, and the council has been explicit about its proposals for stock rationalisation at the local level. Feedback will be given to bidders. The council places a high level of importance on the extent to which RSLs are committed to local areas and their regeneration, and can bring added value in terms of skills and specialisms as well as resources.

The outcome of the process in terms of delivering strategy has yet to be tested in the longer term but some lessons were learnt from the evaluation process. Issues highlighted by the council for future joint commissioning selection processes included the following:
• As with any selection process, the submissions from RSLs did not always reflect known skills.
• The council consultation with members as a part of the selection process needs to be strengthened.
• Tenants and residents were not directly involved in the selection process, but will be involved in the stock rationalisation discussions that follow.

Feedback on the process from RSLs interviewed for the case study was generally good, and the process was felt to have worked quite effectively, although one said that to a large extent RSLs were selected on the basis of where they were already operating with insufficient attention paid to how they were performing.

In the Welland Partnership area, it is hoped that a Partnership-wide development programme can be established as the vehicle for channelling future housing investment in the sub-region (currently authorities are responsible for their own programmes, some through preferred partners and some on the basis of open competition). Partner authorities believe that this approach will assist them in establishing a more strategic approach to planning new development and to meet the needs that authorities have identified (and in particular the need for supported housing). The Partnership has approached the Housing Corporation to begin discussions about the possibility of establishing a Partnership-wide approved development programme:

Figure 21: Case study example: The Welland Partnership and preferred partners

Partnership authorities anticipate working with around six preferred RSL partners, who would be jointly selected. Discussion has not yet taken place on how the selection of preferred partners might take place. However, the Partnership is likely to want to see partner RSLs giving a commitment to bring additional resources to the communities that they will be serving, and it is anticipated that there would be a strong emphasis on criteria such as providing a local management presence and housing management standards/approaches, including a commitment to develop tenant participation arrangements within the wider Partnership Compact.

Partnership authorities are beginning to consider the strategic and management implications of a sub-regional approach to new development. These include:

- the need to establish effective liaison/co-ordination arrangements at county level (the Partnership covers three county councils and one unitary authority)
- the need to address the issue of resource sharing between authorities, and to establish protocols/agreements to govern the distribution of resources over time across the Partnership area
- consideration of how allocations/nominations arrangements need to change to support the common development programme.

Although the approaches being developed by the case study authorities vary, reflecting the differing contexts within which housing strategy is delivered, some clear themes emerge. In particular, there is a strong emphasis on the wider performance of preferred partners, and a determination to incorporate monitoring of general management performance, organisational capacity and adherence to Best Value within development partnerships. There is an expectation that the Housing Corporation will contribute to the process of evaluating the capacity and performance of potential partners, using information gathered through its regulatory role. The authorities hope to develop new approaches to information sharing with the Corporation, to give them access to performance information which has not in the past been directly available.

An important element of the joint commissioning framework is the ability to address grant allocations on a cross-border basis. This fits with the Housing Corporation's commitment to develop a more strategic approach to resource allocation that reflects sub-regional and regional priorities. Some local authorities have already formed partnerships to provide housing across local authority boundaries, including in Cornwall, Suffolk and Hertfordshire. Cross border working has particular benefits for the provision of supported housing, particularly in smaller and rural authorities.

Such approaches depend upon the involvement of RSLs that are able to work in partnership with more than one authority, providing an effective regional and sub-regional dimension.

However, whilst joint commissioning has a number of benefits for local authorities and selected partners, it also has some disadvantages. Some RSLs involved in this study suggested that in focussing on preferred partners, joint commissioning can be too exclusive, and can have a negative impact on those who are not selected. In addition, whilst the joint commissioning process provides a clear framework for partnerships between developing RSLs and local authorities, questions emerge about how the local authority might seek to influence the performance of RSLs that have not been selected as preferred partners, or indeed, those RSLs which are not interested in a development role. We turn now to examine this issue.

Promoting best practice

In Brent there has been an explicit agenda to promote best practice and common approaches to delivering strategic objectives amongst all RSLs (and other organisations involved in providing social housing) through the RSL liaison forum (we look at this in more detail below). In addition, Brent's decision to retain a portion of ADP for allocation outside the joint commissioning process reflects a commitment to enable non-partner RSLs to have development opportunities, and particularly to allow the authority to promote innovative schemes. It is anticipated that such opportunities will give weight to the work of the liaison forum, and the promotion of best practice.

Similarly in the Welland Partnership area there is a commitment to promote best practice, and to develop common approaches to service delivery, where possible.

In Manchester, the authority has adopted a different perspective, with the emphasis placed upon the selection of partners best placed to deliver the council's strategic objectives at the local level, and demonstrating a commitment to those areas. It is expected that such partnerships will be the focus of dialogue about standards and approaches to management. There is an expectation that joint commissioning will support the process of rationalising stock management, and that non-partner RSLs will agree to a transfer of engagements in order to achieve the objectives of more coherent management. However, where non-partners RSLs provide their tenants with a good service, and therefore make a contribution to the area, the council envisages that in some cases they would continue to have a presence. The council is clear that the degree of influence that it is able to have over non-partners will depend ultimately on the extent to which the Housing Corporation is prepared to exert its own influence to support the wider rationalisation programme.

Whilst RSLs interviewed were generally supportive of approaches to share and promote best practice, officers in some of the case study organisations noted that where RSLs work with more than one authority there may be difficulties for them in managing the expectations of local authorities, and in addressing the service delivery and performance monitoring requirements of a range of authorities.

The Best Value regime has particular implications for the nature of relations between RSLs and local authorities. The Housing Corporation expects RSLs to implement Best Value (Housing Corporation, 1999). Although this is not a statutory duty as it is for local authorities, RSL performance is to be externally evaluated through performance indicators and an inspection regime that is comparable with the arrangements for local authorities.

Best Value encompasses a requirement that organisations (local authorities ands RSLs) "benchmark" their performance with that of peer group authorities, to compare both service standards and costs and service delivery approaches. Social housing providers might wish to go further, and reach agreement with local service providers on the approaches to service delivery that best suit the community's needs, and upon the outcomes that social housing providers should aspire to achieve. This is the approach recommended by the LGA task group on the future strategic role (LGA, 2000). It has particular implications in areas where management arrangements within any community are diverse, with a number of landlords serving a single estate for example. Best Value considerations may support the case for shared management arrangements, or other forms of rationalisation.

However, at present there is no particular role for local authorities in influencing the RSL approach to Best Value, other than as one of a number of stakeholders who should be involved in the Best Value review process, and case study authorities have not developed their thinking on the way that this relationship will work. We examine below the possible role that local authorities might play in this respect.

In each of the case study areas, the agenda to influence service standards and service delivery is addressed largely through joint liaison arrangements with RSLs.

Liaison and consultation

Each of the case study areas has an RSL liaison forum in place for the discussion of matters of shared concern, in common with many local authorities. Such forums may also have a role in enabling RSLs to contribute to the development of housing and related strategies, and to oversee the implementation of protocols and working agreements, such as nomination agreements. Increasingly such forums are likely to have a role in promoting best practice and agreeing on shared objectives, although this role is not always explicit. In some areas, liaison between RSLs and local authorities is beginning to focus on the scope for developing common approaches to the provision of landlord services, to providing increased consumer choice in gaining access to housing, and to shared service provision where more than one landlord serves a community.

In the Welland Partnership, the RSL forum is in the very early stages of development, but it has an ambitious agenda for developing common approaches in a number of areas of activity, and for developing a sub-regional framework for issues such as choice-based lettings, shared approaches to stock investment, tenant participation, and housing management standards generally (Appendix 4). The Partnership's plans for joint working on choice-based lettings provide an example both of the cross-border dimension, and the cross-tenure approach that should underpin wider housing strategy:

Figure 22: Case study example: The Welland Partnership and joint working on choice-based lettings.

Developing a common housing register and common approach to allocations are key priorities for the Partnership. Harborough has successfully piloted a choice-based allocations scheme "Homesearch", and the Partnership is keen to draw on this experience and establish a Partnership-wide choice-based approach involving RSLs.

The Partnership's underlying principles concerning cross-border working and arbitrary administrative boundaries are an important motivation for this aspect of work. In the sub-region housing markets do not follow local authority boundaries, and housing providers need to develop more innovative approaches to satisfy housing need. In addition the sub-region is experiencing high demand for affordable housing, and partners hope that the lessons of the Homesearch pilot can be used to improve the efficiency of allocations across the Partnership.

Increasing customer access to and use of IT underpins the partnership's plans and is part of a wider vision to improve access to services and information in rural communities generally through use of IT. A number of initiatives are already underway to make the internet available at access points in villages across the partnership area (including through a Government pilot scheme to provide information access points in rural post offices), and the success of these initiatives is central to the choice-based allocations scheme that is envisaged.

A common housing register already operates between Melton and RSLs, and the Harborough scheme covers all social housing in the borough. The other partners have more conventional points-based systems with nomination arrangements to RSLs. There are therefore major differences that will need to be addressed if a common approach is to be established.

The partnership has made a bid (unsuccessful) for pilot status as part of the Government's choice-based lettings initiative, involving also Longhurst Group, De Montfort Housing Society, Minster General HA, Nene Housing Society, East Midlands HA, Raglan Housing, and the Muir Group. The overarching aim of the initiative is to extend the Harborough Homesearch approach to the entire social rented stock in the sub-region from April 2003. However, the bid assumed an incremental approach, with the next two years being used as follows:

- Provide increased levels of information and publicity for customers about mutual exchange opportunities (a service that will initially be paper based but which will be available on the internet from October 2001).
- Provide increased levels of information on the full range of housing options available across the sub-region, again initially paper based but then available also via the internet.
- Co-ordinate the development of a common approach to allocations between partner authorities and RSLs, and the organisational changes needed to deliver the service, which will involve:
  - developing a work programme to achieve a single Homesearch-based approach to allocations
  - providing training and awareness raising sessions for staff, customers and other stakeholders
  - establishing a single central lettings agency to manage the service on behalf of the partners
  - establishing a Welland Housing Options website
  - establishing an appropriate ITC system to support the service, with a sub-regional property database.

Whilst the pilot bid was unsuccessful, there is still a strong commitment to developing a choice-based approach.

In Brent there is a longstanding liaison group, which is the focus for activities to promote common approaches and raise/address issues of concern (whether by the council or RSLs):

Figure 23: Case study example: The London Borough of Brent and RSL Liaison

An important element of the council's current strategy for exerting influence on RSLs is to facilitate dialogue and share best practice, a process that takes place principally through Brent Housing Group, which meets quarterly. Council officers acknowledged that "influence" is a two way thing, and that RSLs have an interest in using the Housing Group to address aspects of council performance (for example to tackle housing benefit problems and difficulties with the planning process, issues which are discussed further below).

→

Brent Housing Group has five sub-groups that tackle key policy areas: BME strategy, planning, nominations, supported housing and housing benefit. The council feels that these groups operate well and are effective. This was the view also of the RSL officers that we interviewed. The one shortcoming of liaison arrangements mentioned by one RSL representative was the absence of a forum for chief officer liaison – as the Housing Group and sub-group meetings tend to be attended by senior operational staff rather than at director level (although this does depend upon the size of the RSL). It was felt that a periodic chief officer meeting would also be beneficial to facilitate the strategic planning process for both RSLs and the authority. Some RSLs are already involved in the Shadow Local Strategic Partnership, which may fulfil this role.

Together the council and RSLs have been active in using the Housing Group/sub-group structure as a forum to negotiate working arrangements/protocols including:

- Draft partnership protocol between Brent planning department and Brent Housing Group RSLs – designed to specify standard of service provided by planning to RSLs, clarify arrangements for use of s106 agreements, speed up RSL planning applications, encourage dialogue about and establish standards for quality of design and promote achievement of balanced communities. The authority has had a site registration scheme in operation for around 5 years, enabling RSLs to register interest in a site, at which point other applications are put on hold.

- Brent BME Protocol – designed to be incorporated in development agreements where mainstream RSLs act as development agents for BME RSLs, to improve the economy, transparency and fairness of the process (in support of a broader council policy objective that a minimum of 20 per cent of new housing will be made available to BME RSLs).

- Brent nominations agreement – establishes protocol and definitions for administration and monitoring of nominations.

- Shared ownership nomination agreement – designed to increase the number of households in priority needs that are nominated for shared ownership and improve liaison between the council and providers. The authority and RSLs have jointly developed with Northcote Housing Association a database which provides a register of households seeking shared ownership housing.

- Model agreement between Brent Council and RSLs providing temporary accommodation.

- Protocol for dealing with offenders who are a risk to the community (under schedule 1 of the Sex Offenders Act 1997).

- Procedure for dealing with tenants' complaints about disrepair/ mismanagement of temporary accommodation (whether council or RSL is the landlord).

Whilst Brent Housing Group is one way in which the council can seek to promote best practice amongst RSLs and improve collaboration, the Group is viewed by RSLs as a way in which they can seek to influence council performance. The council is aware that some aspects of its performance are of concern to RSLs, and impact upon RSL/scheme viability, including:

- Performance in delivering HB – the ability of RSLs to deliver temporary housing in the private sector is under threat in Brent because of difficulties with housing benefit. The authority is working to address problems with the benefits service, and fears about the loss of temporary accommodation are a driver for this.

- Use of planning powers – the authority is aware of the need to streamline the planning process as far as possible to strengthen the position of RSLs to negotiate, which resulted in the development of the protocol (or service level agreement) described above between Brent Housing Group and the planning department. Planning have now provided a named liaison officer for RSLs, and there has been joint planning/RSL/housing department working on a number of initiatives.

RSLs interviewed for the study raised concerns also about the issue of nominations, and the pressure applied by the authority to maximise the supply of nominations for homeless families. Council officers advise that this is an issue that needs further discussion and development in Brent, as part of the development of the choice-based lettings pilot that is shortly to get underway. Housing officers also expect that the requirement that councils develop a strategy for addressing homelessness (originally to have been introduced under the Homes Bill), will affect relationships with RSLs in meeting housing need. It will be necessary to address the issue of nomination rights and providers' responsibilities as part of the council (and RSL) response to any new legislation.

In Brent, as in many other areas, housing benefit has been a focal point for local authority/RSL liaison. Problems with delivery have frequently undermined other aspects of housing strategy, including the objective of maintaining the supply of private sector housing for rent in areas of high demand, and the viability of high cost/high risk temporary housing schemes (NHF, 2000). Frequently HB is managed by the finance department or corporate teams other than housing, and may not be addressed as an element of housing strategy. Therefore, whilst the relationship between other corporate services (such as planning, social services and environmental health) and housing strategy is generally addressed within strategy statements, the role of HB may not be considered (see for example CIH, 1998 and LGA, 2001 where local authority strategy statements' coverage of the subject is not mentioned).

Just as approaches to the delivery of the benefit affect the performance of local authority landlord services (a fact acknowledged by the HIP appraisal process), they also affect RSL performance, and the wider operation of the private rented sector. Authorities are recommended to develop service level agreements with RSLs on the issue (NHF, 2000). It is important that local authorities acknowledge the impact of housing benefit administration upon the delivery of housing strategy, and engage landlords in all sectors to ensure that benefit services support wider housing strategy.

The implications of rent restructuring have not yet become a focal point of liaison arrangements between authorities and RSLs, but are likely to do so in the coming years. Whilst there will be limited scope for influencing the outcome of the rent restructuring process, other than in decisions on use of the 5 per cent tolerance that is permitted to reflect local considerations, authorities are likely to wish to examine with RSLs the impact of revised rent levels on affordability, and upon demand and RSL viability, and the capacity of the sector as a whole.

Liaison also takes place between RSLs and local authorities at an individual level, or focussed on estates/communities with common issues. As with more formal liaison forums, this may have a reactive agenda, to deal with problems and concerns as they come up, or may be prompted by initiatives to share good practice, benchmark performance and promote common approaches to management. For example, Rutland County Council and Nene Housing Association have been working together to benchmark performance for their stock within the county.

The stock transfer sector

Both the London Borough of Brent and Manchester City Council have extensive experience of partial stock transfer (see Appendices 2 & 3).

In these authorities, there are considerable differences in the relationships between local authorities and RSLs in the LSVT and traditional (non LSVT) sectors, as follows:

a) RSL partners are commonly selected through a competitive process, or are established by the transferring local authority. This gives the local authority the opportunity to influence the shape of the organisation, and to define the way that relationships with the authority will work, to the extent permitted by the Housing Corporation (whilst local authorities are able to use their influence to shape the new organisation, once up and running the new RSL [and its board] has to demonstrate that its independence).

b) Local authority nominees (generally elected members) hold up to a third of seats on the RSL Board, and the sponsoring council may control a portion of the organisation's membership, and through this has the ability to veto changes to the governing articles.

c) Transfer agreements operate between the council, the RSL (and where relevant also with the parent RSL) governing issues such as adherence to commitments to tenants, and arrangements for nominations and decants.

d) Local authorities may monitor aspects of RSL performance, and in particular progress with refurbishment/redevelopment/demolition programmes, business plan implementation and nominations performance.

The rationale for such intervention focuses on protecting the interests of former council tenants, and ensuring that express commitments (for example with regard to regeneration programmes) are met. Local authority nominees have the opportunity to influence the governance of the new organisation and ensure that commitments to tenants are met.

Some LSVT RSL officers commented that local authority board membership has been problematic; attendance levels tended to be poorer than for other categories of board member and vacancies tended to remain unfilled for long periods. There was a view that for council nominees, the responsibilities of board membership take second place to the responsibilities of council membership. We are aware that in at least one local authority with a large-scale programme of partial stock transfer, local authority officers have been invited to become local authority nominees on RSL boards, and that this was felt to have been beneficial from the RSL perspective.

Council officers in one of the case study authorities commented that LSVT RSL board membership is viewed as an issue for local politicians, rather than an issue for strategic management by council officers. Board membership is not viewed as a mechanism for influencing the governance or operations of partners RSLs.

As noted above, neither Brent nor Manchester had sought to apply similar approaches to intervention to the traditional RSL sector (although Brent Council does have nominees on the boards of some traditional RSLs).

Some council officers were of the view that the relationship between the council and LSVT RSLs would change over time (as regeneration programmes come to an end), and would become more akin to the relationships that exist with traditional RSLs.

Redefining roles and responsibilities

We noted at the start of this chapter that new definitions of the strategic housing role are underpinned by an expectation that authorities will intervene to influence the capacity and operation of the RSL sector (as one element of the wider housing market).

Our discussions in all case study areas revealed wide (although not total) acceptance amongst local authority and RSL officers of the principle of local authority involvement in promoting best practice amongst RSLs, and in seeking to develop common approaches that meet local requirements. This is accompanied by an assumption that local authority monitoring of RSL activities will need to be developed. Case study authorities are to varying degrees beginning to address this role, although conscious of the limitations on their ability to influence RSL activity. At present, however, local authorities are doing little to monitor the performance of RSLs (except in the case of LSVT organisations and joint commissioning partners) and there are concerns about how data can be shared and monitored without imposing unnecessary, additional bureaucracy for all concerned.

There is also an interest in developing local authority influence over the grant allocations process, through the joint commissioning process. But again, there is concern to avoid creating a duplication of roles. If local authorities are to play a more active part in influencing the operation of the sector, in order to deliver their wider strategic responsibilities, there will be a need to clarify the respective roles and relationships of both parties.

Current Housing Corporation/Local Authority roles

Local authorities have no express regulatory powers with regard to RSLs other than:

a) as part of their general responsibilities for tackling dis-repair and the condition of housing across all tenures

b) through the grant giving function, to which conditions may be attached

c) where housing or land has been transferred, with conditions attached.

RSLs are independent, non-profit distributing bodies, controlled by governing boards, which have responsibility for ensuring that RSLs operate in accordance with the requirements of statute, external regulators, and other stakeholders (for a full discussion of the regulatory arrangements for RSLs, see NHF, 1999). Many RSLs operate across local authority boundaries and have to manage relationships with a wide range of agencies across their areas of operation.

The Housing Corporation is the principal regulator of RSLs, and has a wide range of general and specific powers to influence their operation. The primary regulatory mechanism is that of registration, through which applicants are required to demonstrate their capacity to comply with the "Performance Standards" that RSLs are expected to achieve. RSLs need the consent of the Corporation before certain actions can be taken (for example, to dispose of land, change the rules governing the organisation's operation or merge with another organisation). Compliance with Corporation expectations is monitored through a range of mechanisms, including submission of quarterly and annual returns and periodic inspection. The Corporation also has a range of enforcement powers.

The Corporation is also responsible for ensuring that RSLs implement Best Value. The Corporation has established a separate Best Value division which will be responsible for reviewing the performance of RSLs. The Corporation will shortly be issuing guidance on the way that its approach to regulation will change, to reflect the demands of Best Value. It is proposed that this will focus on a new Regulatory Code, setting out the fundamental obligations of RSLs, supported by separately identified statutory and regulatory guidance. Linked to this, the Corporation is responsible for ensuring that RSLs consult and empower residents, in accordance with its Performance Standards framework.

The Housing Corporation is also responsible for the allocation of capital and revenue funds to RSLs, and for ensuring that housing investment contributes to wider national policy objectives. The investment and regulatory elements of the Corporation role are closely related. RSLs cannot expect to receive social housing grant unless their performance meets adequate standards (as set out within the Performance Assessment Investment Summary, a confidential report of RSL suitability for receiving grant produced by the Housing Corporation).

If the local authority role in influencing the RSL sector is to be extended, a re-appraisal of the respective roles of local authorities and the Housing Corporation will be required. In the past, local authorities have had a limited role in the investment process, in helping to shape regional investment plans, through their assessment of local housing needs, and also through the allocation of local authority social housing grant (LASHG). However, they have not had a specific responsibility for evaluating/monitoring RSL performance either in respect of investment or performance generally (although some local authorities do seek performance information from prospective partner/partner RSLs).

There are some difficulties involved in establishing performance monitoring arrangements at a local level:

- RSLs are required to produce regulatory and performance information for the Housing Corporation. They are not always able to disaggregate information at a local authority level, or in the ways that local authorities require (or are only able to meet local authority requirements by carrying out laborious manual exercises to produce performance data in the required format). The Housing Corporation produces an analysis of RSL performance information by local authority, which is supplied to local authorities in the form of an annual report. However, this information takes time to reach publication and has limited value in making assessments of RSL performance.

- Local authorities have not in the past had automatic access to much of the regulatory and performance information held by the Housing Corporation, either in relation to the investment process or performance generally (although RSLs can be asked to provide information, as a condition of grant or when competing for preferred partner status).

Things are changing however. Some RSLs have been working to improve the quality and timeliness of data that can be made available to individual authorities about their performance in specific areas. The development of the HouseMark Local service is an example of this. The G15 group of (London based) RSLs has been working with HouseMark to enable RSL data to be disaggregated to local level, allowing RSLs to compare their performance with peer group RSLs operating within particular localities. This will be of value both to local authorities and RSLs themselves. (It is anticipated that the service will be used to examine trends in rent collection and arrears, which will in turn aid RSLs' monitoring of housing benefit administration in different local authority areas).

The Housing Corporation is taking steps to increase the amount of previously confidential information about RSLs that can be made available to local authorities and other stakeholders. Sixty of the country's largest RSLs are having their Performance Assessment Investment Summary reports published on the internet on a pilot basis, giving stakeholders access to information about organisational and financial health, and general housing management performance. These reports will be updated through the year, as regulatory and performance reports become available, providing more up to date information about RSL performance than is otherwise available. The success of the pilot will be reviewed, before a decision is taken on whether to extend the project to other groups of RSLs.

In addition, joint commissioning has strengthened the degree of collaboration and information sharing between local authorities and the Corporation in areas where the approach has been adopted, and has facilitated the development of longer term planning to meet investment needs. The Government wishes to see the approach extended. However, as noted above it has been suggested that local authorities may be given opportunities for still greater involvement in the investment process where they have transferred their stock.

Thus, through an evolutionary process, the boundaries between the roles of the Housing Corporation and local authorities are changing, and at different rates and in different ways from area to area. This study predominantly concentrates on the relationship between local authorities and RSLs, rather than the relationship of either with the Corporation. However, any development of the local authority strategic and enabling role must have implications for the Corporation's activities, especially given the widened remit of RSLs.

Whilst it is not within the remit of this study to consider the Corporation's long-term role, it is worth noting that, for a number of reasons, the process of transferring RSL-related responsibilities from the Corporation to local authorities is almost certainly finite. Even if all local authorities (whether individually or in sub-regional or regional groupings) were able to take on the strategic and enabling roles in full, the nature of the sector still provides an arguably strong case for a national regulator and, indeed, funding agency. The following are the principal reasons:

a) The RSL sector needs national certain absolute standards of governance and financial regulation (e.g. audit, duality of interest, form of accounts).

b) The sector also needs minimum service performance standards even if local diversity is encouraged.

c) The viability of the sector is dependent on the continuing confidence of private funders, much of which is based on centralised regulation and the consequent ability (including the exercise of statutory powers) to deal with major problems.

d) Key stakeholders, like funders, usefully have a national, statutory agency to and from whom representations can be made; this is a distinct role from that of the representative bodies such as the National Housing Federation.

e) Central government may wish to maintain a route for ensuring that spending and other policy priorities are delivered across the country.

f) A central agency is arguably even more necessary given the continuing growth of the sector. Even if more rationalisation is achieved – and especially if this is through sub-regional and regional group structures – the necessary influence over the sector can never solely be delivered through local authorities.

The way forward

The LGA has suggested that there is a need to review the relationship between councils and RSLs to reflect the changing context (LGA, 2000). They propose that local authorities and RSLs should adopt a new form of local agreement that addresses:

- their shared strategic and operational objectives
- their respective roles and responsibilities
- common performance standards and targets (incorporating qualitative issues)
- arrangements for sharing information
- operational plans on matters such as common allocations and local lettings schemes
- common approaches to tenant participation
- common approaches to monitoring performance
- common objectives on rents and affordability (LGA, 2000).

The LGA, the NHF and the Housing Corporation are in the process of developing a model framework document to assist local authorities and RSLs in working together more effectively to deliver housing strategy, taking account of the new demands of the strategic housing role. Such a document should assist strategic housing authorities to review their relationships with RSLs and to develop a more strategic approach.

We set out below the key principles that might underpin any such agreement:

- A greater role for LAs should not increase the burden of regulation for RSLs; it should be achieved by:
  - greater information sharing (with the continuation and extension of the PAIS pilot, and giving local authorities access to on-line information about scheme progress and performance against targets)
  - development of standardised approaches to gathering local authority level data
  - a clear allocation of roles for the Housing Corporation and local authorities respectively (rather than the duplication of responsibilities).
- The focus of local authority activity should be upon:
  - assessing the capacity and monitoring the performance of all RSLs within their area (not just developing RSLs), or where working in collaboration with other authorities, within the sub-region
  - assessing the impact of RSL activities upon specific communities
  - encouraging best practice and continuous improvement in RSL performance through information sharing and monitoring
  - monitoring the success of preferred partners in delivering agreed objectives
  - sharing this information with the Housing Corporation to improve the regulator's understanding of the impact of RSL activities at a local level.
- The focus of Housing Corporation activity would be:
  - RSL-wide performance, and organisational and financial health
  - ensuring that local authorities are kept informed through the PAIS report mechanism and other available means about overall concerns and areas of weakness
  - sole responsibility for regulation and Best Value inspection.
- The tools used by local authorities and the Housing Corporation will be determined by the remit described above, for example:

– The Housing Corporation will continue to gather data for the organisation as a whole, to evaluate overall organisational and financial health and the achievement of national policy objectives. To support the local planning process, the Corporation should support the use of the HouseMark benchmarking system, developed by the Chartered Institute of Housing and Arthur Andersen, as the basis of producing standard data outputs by RSLs and local authorities. The Corporation should also support the use by RSLs of the HouseMark Local system, developed at the behest of the largest London RSLs, which enables RSLs to disaggregate performance data at local authority level.

– The local authority will identify local information needs, in collaboration with RSLs, focussing on key performance indicators and outcomes that enable the authority to evaluate the impact of the service on consumers and the achievement of local housing strategy.

The principles identified above are based upon the presumption that the Housing Corporation retains primary responsibility for development allocations and monitoring the investment function. Were this situation to change, as the Government has proposed, the extent of local authority responsibility in relation to the investment process would also need to change, with local authorities assuming a greater share of responsibility for making investment decisions and evaluating RSLs' success in delivering schemes at local level, and the Housing Corporation providing contextual information through its regulatory role concerning the overall performance of the organisation.

Building upon the principles set out above, local authorities should address the need to promote best practice, and Best Value, amongst all providers of social housing in the area. This should include developing/preferred partner RSLs as well as non-partner/non-developing RSLs, and also local authority owned providers. Indeed, authorities need to address ways of establishing effective partnerships with non-developing RSLs, whose potential contribution to the achievement of strategy needs also to be considered. The "agreement" based approach proposed by the LGA task group would provide a basis for this. Effective liaison and joint working arrangements will be essential to underpin such agreements.

Authorities should consider how they will address a monitoring role that extends to all RSLs. We would suggest that two tiers of monitoring are required. The first for developing RSLs should focus on how they perform in delivering the outputs and outcomes required by funding/partnership agreements (and should be fully integrated with Corporation monitoring arrangements). The extent of local authority responsibility in this respect could be linked to the extent of separation from the provider function. A second regime could operate for all RSLs including non-developing RSLs. We would endorse the suggestion from some RSLs involved in this study that such monitoring should focus on broad outcomes such as customer satisfaction with housing services, and should draw on the standard performance information data that RSLs are now required to produce. A challenge for all social housing providers will be to disaggregate data to neighbourhood level, to allow for an examination of the way that communities are served. As noted above, we recommend that the Housing Corporation supports the HouseMark benchmarking system to promote standardised approaches to the production of data.

Finally, authorities should ensure that RSL tenants have full access to opportunities for involvement and participation. This should include:

- providing opportunities for RSL tenants' participation in Community and Housing Strategy development (in collaboration with RSLs)
- encouraging RSLs to consult their tenants effectively, and monitoring their performance in this respect
- working with RSLs to establish shared consultation arrangements in multi-landlord communities.

We turn now to address the way in which the principles described above might be used by local housing authorities to influence the capacity of the RSL sector to deliver strategic housing objectives.

5 | Influencing the capacity and shape of the RSL sector

Should local authorities seek to influence the shape of the sector?

The question of whether and how local authorities should seek to influence the shape of the RSL sector is prompted by a number of factors (see chapter 2):

- concerns that there are too many RSLs operating in some neighbourhoods
- concerns that RSL stock is too widely scattered and the suggestion that they should concentrate their activities on core areas
- the expectation that rent-restructuring and other pressures will force more RSLs to consider merger or stock rationalisation in order to remain viable.

We examined these concerns during our discussions with case study organisations. In each case study area, relatively large numbers of RSLs manage the stock portfolio (particularly in Brent), whilst a much smaller core of RSLs have active development programmes, and more active partnerships with their respective local authorities:

Figure 24: RSL presence in the case study areas

Case study authority	No. of RSLs	No. of developing RSLs***	No. of RSL units****
Brent	56*	15	11,806
Manchester	53**	11	25,894
Rutland	9*	4	240

(Source: * Housing Corporation and information from officers; ** information from officers; *** 2000/01 ADP summary; **** HIP Operational Information 2000.)

We asked case study organisations for their views on the question of the need for rationalisation, and the role that local authorities might play.

Figure 25: Case study example: The London Borough of Brent and the future shape of the sector

There has not been any formal discussion within Brent about stock rationalisation. Generally, officers do not have concerns about the diversity of the sector, although it was felt that a "rationalised" sector (i.e. with fewer RSLs) would be easier to manage. However, in Brent diversity is encouraged, and the council is continuing to promote opportunities for non-partner RSLs to bring forward individual schemes within the broader preferred partner framework. Similarly great emphasis is placed on promoting the involvement of small BME RSLs through transfers of the management and ownership of new homes. Diversity is therefore built into the system in Brent. One small BME RSL interviewed for the study raised concerns about how Housing Corporation statements on stock rationalisation can be reconciled with the promotion of BME RSLs. Council officers also commented that the two strategies are difficult to reconcile.

→

Plans for joint commissioning in Brent have not included proposals for zoning (i.e. allocating specific areas to specific RSLs), as has been the case elsewhere, although there has been informal discussion about this.

In terms of taking steps to exert influence over the shape of the sector, for example through stock rationalisation or merger, the authority feels that it has limited influence, particularly with regard to substantial RSLs with portfolios that extend well beyond Brent. RSLs interviewed for the study suggested that councils might have a useful role to play in co-ordinating dialogue about the shape of the sector in their areas, particularly against the backdrop of rent-restructuring, and possibly in acting as a broker in merger talks, but there was a strong view that it would be inappropriate for local authorities to seek specifically to influence ownership arrangements or the outcome of merger talks.

A number of mergers have taken place involving RSLs operating in Brent, but the council's experience is that is unlikely to be the first to know about merger proposals (although it is more likely to be kept informed by development partners), even where merger is prompted by an RSL getting into difficulty. The authority has not formulated a view on the role it would like to play, and sees the sector as dependent upon the Housing Corporation to take the lead in merger/rationalisation negotiations.

Figure 26: Case study example: Manchester City Council and the future shape of the sector

Manchester City Council views the rationalisation of the management of the social housing sector as central to the longer term delivery of corporate housing strategy. The council is clear that the degree of influence that the council can have over the stock rationalisation will depend ultimately on the influence that the Housing Corporation wishes to exert. Working relationships with the Housing Corporation are very good, and the HC is fully committed to the stock rationalisation plans in the city.

All RSLs interviewed were of the view that there were too many RSLs operating across the city. The large number is felt to undermine the council's strategic ability, particularly in areas where complex regeneration programmes were required or being delivered. One RSL commented that getting anything done was difficult because so many RSLs had to be consulted and at any one time at least 50 per cent would be bound to disagree with council plans. There were felt to be some strengths with the current profile however, including:

- the large number means there is a broad cross section of (financially) strong RSLs, so that if any one RSL fails the implications across the city will be less severe than in a "rationalised" sector
- from residents' and applicants' perspective, the large number promoted choice of landlord.

A comment repeated more than once was that the council could have been tougher on stock rationalisation much earlier. RSLs described the discussions as having taken place over many years. However, the extent to which the council could exert real pressure was acknowledged to be limited.

Both the council and the RSLs interviewed appear to agree that the real underlying issue is the number of diverse management arrangements in any one area rather than the ownership of the stock, although the council's proposals were clearly seen by RSLs as an intention to change the ownership of the stock in the pilot areas.

The most significant issue for the outcome of the stock rationalisation discussions was perceived by RSLs to be the council's future intentions on further transfers of its own stock. This was regarded as likely to increase competition to some degree – one commented that this would also extend to competition for independent board members, as much as in stock and service delivery issues. Where the council has plans for a major stock transfer the joint commissioning proposals are explicitly short to medium term.

Rent restructuring proposals are also expected by the council to have significant impact on the shape of the sector, and the number of active RSLs, but it is considered difficult at present to predict what the impact will be. RSLs were also reticent about the likely impact. One commented that whilst the logical expectation would be that more mergers would take place, in previous times of constraint on RSLs similar expectations have been expressed but have not ultimately materialised.

Figure 27: Case study example: The Welland Partnership and the future shape of the sector

Thoughts on stock rationalisation are in the very early stages of development, and are not formally on the strategy agenda. Further, it is not yet clear to what extent stock transfer will be on the agenda of the four authorities that have not gone done the transfer route to date. However, the housing group believes that for some communities within the sub-region where a number of landlords have stock holdings there may be advantages in exploring rationalisation. Officers are committed to the principle that what matters is what works; and that both councils and RSLs should be prepared to enter into discussions about which agencies should continue to have a role in ownership/management in the longer term.

RSL officers interviewed for the study were more cautious about the rationalisation issue, and about the role that local authorities should play. One officer commented that rationalisation, whether of ownership or management, is a matter for RSLs themselves. However, there was also a view that there "are too many RSLs" operating in the partnership area, and that rationalisation should be on the agenda.

RSLs found it difficult to comment on the possible implications of further transfers of local authority housing, although one officer noted that traditional RSLs fear their role may be undermined by the creation of substantial new RSLs to receive transfers of council housing.

Views on the need for rationalisation vary considerably, reflecting to a degree the extent to which intervention in the market is perceived as necessary to deliver strategic objectives. And this is in our view an essential starting point for any debate about rationalisation; to what extent is intervention required to deliver strategic objectives?

Influencing the capacity of the sector to deliver strategic objectives

It is questionable whether local authorities will be able, successfully, to carry out the strategic housing role as it is now defined without fully understanding the profile of the sector, and considering the extent to which landlords, individually and as a whole, are capable of meeting local requirements. This implies that local authorities should have a role in influencing the shape and operation of the sector (in addition to an understanding of how RSLs are performing). In our view, any discussion about local authority intervention in the shape of the sector must be placed firmly within the context of the capacity of the sector to meet local requirements and be based on clear objectives. These should include capacity to improve management, ensure strategic RSL capacity locally and ensure a diversity of providers and a "market" in terms of relevant local factors.

We turn now to consider the different models of intervention that would enable strategic housing authorities to deliver their objectives. The models we consider may be summarised as follows:

a) directive

b) open market

c) managed market.

We describe each in turn together with its advantages and disadvantages.

Directive

Nationally, the track record of the RSL sector in achieving voluntary stock ownership rationalisation is poor. Thus, the corollary of the view that stock ownership should be rationalised is that some element of compulsion is needed. This in turn suggests a possible role for the local authority which as the body with the responsibility for ensuring that the pattern of provision meets local needs, should be able to direct the compulsory transfer of management and/or ownership of RSL homes to other RSLs.

Such a directive approach, in order to achieve the aim of rationalisation, would also have to include the power to determine which RSLs received funding for housing-related purposes (e.g. from the Housing Corporation and through SRB or New Deal for Communities schemes with a housing element).

The advantages of this approach are as follows:

a) The Housing Corporation and LAs fund and give other support to the RSL sector, and LAs increasingly rely on RSLs to meet a wide range of social housing, community care and regeneration objectives. These facts, and the substantial funding that goes into the sector, mean that it is essential that the work of RSLs is co-ordinated and focussed on strategically important issues. Whilst RSLs are legally outside the public sector, their existence and growth is wholly dependent on their historic asset base (in most cases accumulated through substantial capital grants) and future (and increasing) public funding.

b) It may be perceived that given the failure of exhortation to achieve significant RSL stock rationalisation in the past, a compulsory approach is the only way likely to guarantee significant change.

c) Local authorities, particularly if they give up the landlord role, have few direct controls over social housing provision and management. However, they retain the responsibility for ensuring an effective housing strategy; if the CIH and LGA proposals are implemented, this will be a legal requirement with the risk of legal or financial sanctions if an authority does not perform adequately. However, there are no major sanctions, particularly upon an RSL that does not need or want development funding, against ignoring an authority's strategic needs.

d) If the Housing Corporation were to have the right to be consulted before any compulsory transfer or limitation of funding, in order to take a wider view in relation to regional provision and the viability of the sector, this would prevent excessively parochial, or unfairly discriminatory, proposals by authorities.

e) This power might well only rarely be used but its existence could provide a greater incentive both to RSL stock transfers or other restructuring (e.g. mergers or the creation of group structures).

The disadvantages of this approach are as follows:

a) The RSL sector is, and will remain for the foreseeable future, a market of independent, but regulated, non-profit distributing bodies. The very independence of the sector means, however, that it cannot be reorganised to some agreed blueprint, even if it were possible to conceive of such a thing. The public sector has, indeed, provided substantial funding to the sector but this has knowingly been to bodies that are independent of it. Funding has been consciously given in pursuit of pluralism and on the basis that the involvement of values-based, independent organisations, historically with voluntary board membership, is important. Such funding would be unsustainable were RSL assets to be (as it would be seen) confiscated.

b) Decisions on stock rationalisation may well not be demonstrably objective. To confiscate assets on the basis of a judgement on the "right" number of RSLs will often, if not always, be arbitrary.

c) This process also is essentially input – rather than outcome – driven. If an RSL is managing well a few properties distant from its base why should they be compelled to give them up?

d) A process that rationalises RSL stockholding to a preferred template almost inevitably ignores the views of the individual tenants concerned.

e) Losing stock may undermine the financial viability of RSLs. This would inevitably raise the need for compensation, both source and amount.

This suggests that a full-scale directive approach is not feasible, specifically if it includes compulsory transfer of existing stock. Giving local authorities more power to decide which RSLs receive any housing-related funding in their area (not just from the Housing Corporation) may well be desirable, and a useful addition to the enabling role. Giving *RSL tenants*, rather than local authorities, the power to initiate management reviews by the Housing Corporation may be a way of providing more incentives to better management, which is arguably a more important objective than rationalisation per se.

Open market

In many areas of government provision, a relatively open market operates in that services or products are procured on a competitive basis albeit often from a select list of suitably experienced tenderers. To some extent, the RSL sector works within this setting. Increasingly, and with encouragement from central government, opportunities such as stock transfer or regeneration schemes are opened up to wide competition rather than offered to approved RSLs. The case study authorities have used such approaches. To some extent, social housing grant is allocated on some "open market" factors (e.g. amount of grant required and cost of schemes).

This begs the question whether an open market approach could be extended across the range of RSL activities (for example through open competition for all commissioned services and grant-aided provision) and whether this would help or hinder the achievement of local authorities' strategic aims.

The advantages of this approach are as follows:

a) Local authorities would test the market to ensure value for money and quality on all aspects on the work of RSL including cross-tenure services.

b) Providing the factors used were sufficiently broad, the competitive process would drive up quality and could flexibly reflect tenants' and other service users' concerns.

c) A highly competitive approach would arguably encourage stock rationalisation and the restructuring of the sector.

The disadvantages of this approach are as follows:

a) This makes it difficult to involve RSLs in planning and the development of strategies as actual partners will not be known at that stage.

b) Certain types of RSLs (e.g. black and minority ethnic) may find it difficult to compete but may have a crucial strategic role to play.

c) This approach plays little or no attention, and offers nothing, to non-developing RSLs.

d) It provides little incentive for RSLs to devote research and development time to initiatives from which they have no guaranteed return.

Whilst elements of this approach are likely to continue to have merit, a wholly open market approach does not provide a credible basis for planning and partnership, both of which are essential to carry out the strategic and enabling roles.

Managed market

The case study authorities, and particularly Brent and Manchester, are effectively at present trying to manage the market of RSLs. Whether reluctantly or not, they acknowledge the independence of the RSL sector and their lack of direct controls. By and large, they are working collaboratively with skilled and sympathetic RSLs, and have good relations with the Housing Corporation. This suggests that a "managed market" approach is the right way to continue. In a managed market, the authority has clear strategic aims and will use whatever statutory and contractual powers at its disposal to direct or regulate players which will include RSLs. However, it will principally rely on its influence through planning mechanisms, the awarding of funding or other material benefits, by advocacy (e.g. acting as consumer champion) and by dissemination of information (e.g. on good practice and performance). It will also seek to negotiate with and otherwise influence other key players (e.g. the Housing Corporation). Under a managed market, with more systematic benchmarking, and the publication of performance indicators, quasi-market pressures to restructure/merge RSLs and/or rationalise management are likely to emerge.

Given that this approach follows current best practice, it is in a sense "more of the same". However, there is a case for saying that the current enabling role pays insufficient attention to assessing the nature and capacity of the RSL sector.

To meet the aims of the "managed market", the RSL sector in any local authority area will need to have the following characteristics:

a) Sufficient capacity within existing housing stock and through investment (including in new provision, demolition and remodelling) to meet targets for the affordable housing supply.

b) The ability to provide effective and efficient management of the stock.

c) The ability to contribute to alleviating homeless and responding to other initiatives that need quick and flexible responses (e.g. housing asylum seekers).

d) The ability to contribute beyond the social housing sector, particularly to assist weak or changing housing markets.

e) The ability to support vulnerable people to live independent lives.

f) The ability to mitigate poverty and social exclusion.

g) The ability to create safe and thriving communities, not simply satisfactory individual homes, through effective management.

h) Committed to giving individuals maximum choice and influence over their lives.

i) Committed to being accountable.

j) Conscious of the contribution housing makes to good health, reflecting this in its work.

k) Aware of and responsive to the need to protect the environment and maximise the use of sustainable resources.

l) In all the above, willing and able to plan and deliver in partnership with others.

The significance of each of these factors may differ between local authority areas. Not every RSL needs to be able to respond fully to each factor. However, within any local authority area, the LA needs to have sufficient and suitable RSLs to meet these strategic objectives to the extent required.

The chart on the following pages seeks to identify under each characteristic the aims to be achieved and the methods or mechanics that the local authority can use to make its assessment.

Figure 28: Evaluating the capacity of the RSL sector to deliver housing strategy

Characteristic	Aim	Mechanics
1 Capacity of existing stock/ investment capacity	Dwelling number and mix which match projected need. Where surpluses or deficits existing, sufficient financial and capacity skills to develop/demolish/ remodel and to keep existing/retained stock in good condition.	Housing demand projection. RSL stock profile analysis. RSL funding capacity profiles. Demolition/development targets compared to capacity.
2 Effective management	Management standards and approaches comply with Housing Corporation regulatory requirements and Best Value performance plan targets, and are capable of delivering locally agreed target outcomes.	PAIS Report. Best Value Performance Reports and PIs. Benchmarking. Customer satisfaction surveys.
3 Homelessness/ responsiveness	Access to sufficient housing to meet expected homelessness levels. Strategies for responding to unexpected, large demand (e.g. civil emergency, asylum seekers) and an assessment of this capacity.	Temporary accommodation. – directly available stock or methods of acquiring (e.g. private sector leasing schemes). Turnover rates.
4 Other tenures	Expertise and mechanisms to intervene successfully within the private owner occupied and rented sector to meet weaknesses in management, maintenance, long-term investment and financing.	Care and repair operations. PRS support operations. Private sector leasing.
5 Vulnerable people independence	Expertise to meet "ordinary life" principles i.e. to enable everyone to live as independently as possible maximising use of facilities within the community rather than specialist services.	Care and support staff or established partnership arrangements. →

Characteristic	Aim	Mechanics
6 Mitigate poverty and social exclusion	Levy charges that are affordable by low paid households. Produce homes that minimise other outgoings especially on fuel and water. Have systems to identify and address discriminatory practices and behaviour in all aspects of housing.	Affordable rent policy. Energy/resource efficiency/fuel poverty strategies. Equal opportunities policies and monitoring.
7 Safe and secure estates	Minimise crime and fear of crime. Development that is secure by design.	Policies on community safety and anti-social behaviour.
8 Individual choice and influence	Choice of landlords throughout the LA area. Provide a range of opportunities for tenants/consumers to influence policy, practice and decisions through all aspects of work.	Avoidance of monopoly or dominant landlords but balanced against need for development capacity and viable RSLs. Clear LA view on "minimum standard" and "best practice" governance arrangements.
9 Accountable	Ensure maximum transparency of decision-making.	Openness policies.
10 Health	Build and manage to encourage good health. Facilitate support to maximise healthy lifestyles.	Level of environmental health action within RSL sector. Health audits.
11 Environment and sustainable resources	Add to the quality of the environment. Maximise use of sustainable resources.	Contribution to LA's environmental policies and targets – setting and implementation.
12 Willingness to work in partnership	Clear understanding of skills and limitations, and credible ways of filling gaps through partnership.	Capability audits.

Many local authorities do not quantify clearly what contribution they expect the RSL sector to make to meeting their housing objectives. Whilst the Housing Corporation has greatly improved its consultation of local authorities on investment, local authorities are often in a reactive position, responding to schemes identified by RSLs. When local authorities have their own major schemes to promote (e.g. stock transfers or New Deal projects) they have no sound basis on which to choose the appropriate partner. They may have general, anecdotal views on capacity or specialisms, but they have no systematic basis for making selections. The conventional bidding process, not the least because of pressures of time, does not necessarily provide a firm basis for choice of a partner. This leaves local authorities uncertain and can waste the time and energies of RSLs who put forward proposals only to be told (for example) that they are judged not to have the necessary skills or financial capacity.

Local authorities have tended to favour the creation of new RSLs to receive stock transfers, and to parcel transfers so that new landlords become dominant providers in the locality. Given that many local authorities already have large numbers of operational RSLs to choose from, it is debatable whether it is appropriate to create new RSLs in such cases. Indeed, DETR are now insisting that authorities look at all landlord options with tenants when considering transfer of all or part of their stock (DETR, 2000h). Local authorities should be using an evaluation of the capacity of the sector to help determine how best to structure the stock transfer process, in collaboration with residents.

Housing strategies may show the level of nominations expected to RSLs but do not generally include long term forecasts of the capacity required from the sector. Similarly, local authority housing strategies often list the RSLs operating in the area but do not include an assessment of the skills needed to meet strategic objectives. Where the local authority identifies gaps, filling them is often an ad hoc process, sometimes arbitrarily determined (e.g. a new RSL promotes itself to a local authority).

Local authorities do little generally to build capacity within the RSL sector and most would probably not see themselves as having this role. The Housing Corporation, as RSL regulator, has a clearer remit in shaping the structure of the sector but has traditionally been reluctant to restructure – or even be seen to encouraging restructuring – whether through merger, the creation of group structures or by other partnerships. The Corporation has recently recommitted itself to a "light touch" regulatory approach, and this is to be welcomed. However, there is a potential – probably actual – vacuum between the increased role of the RSL sector in delivering local authority strategies (housing and other) and the absence of any real leverage on the part of local authorities over the sector.

Giving local authorities influence over the shape of the sector is problematic as most developing RSLs work in more than one local authority area, although the significance of this may reduce as stock transfers increase, creating more large landlords focussed (even if not solely operating) in one area. Local authorities are not, however, necessarily well served in the long term by working largely with RSLs solely concentrating in their area, despite the superficial attraction of greater local authority influence. A wide range of skills, innovative approaches, more efficient procurement and a stronger asset base may be available from a broader-based RSL or RSL group/partnership.

It may therefore be in the interests of a local authority (or group of local authorities) to seek to influence the shape of the RSL sector operating in its area in a more coherent way than at present. Such changes, given the independence of RSLs, the role of the Housing Corporation and the spirit of partnership will need to be planned jointly and implemented with agreement and incentives. As noted above, local benchmarking may generate pressures for merger/stock rationalisation, placing the local authority at the centre of discussions about how best to manage change. Local authorities need to be free to decide that a "managed market" approach to RSL activity is strategically right for their area; similarly, individual RSLs need to be able to opt out of joint planning (albeit with implications for the extent of local authority or other public funding and pressure from tenants for a review of management arrangements should standards of performance be allowed to drop).

Under this model, on a (say) 3-5 yearly cycle, every local authority should be required to produce an "RSL Expectations Statement". This should itemise and quantify what the local authority is seeking from the RSL sector over a 3-5 year rolling period bearing in mind its strategic objectives and targets. This should be expressed in terms of:

a) indicators of effective, and improving, housing management

b) volume of contribution to meeting demand including from homeless households

c) volume of contribution to reducing inappropriate supply

d) interventions in the private sector – nature and amount

e) provision of housing with care and support

f) nature and extent of contribution to regeneration.

As a document, this will express the "demand" side of the RSL sector equation. The local authority, in collaboration with local operating RSLs, should then produce an "RSL Capacity Statement", analysing the extent to which RSLs operating in the area can meet the requirement of the Expectations Statement. The Housing Corporation could play the role of "auditor" of the Capacity Statement to help the local authority be assured of a balanced and accurate picture. RSLs should be encouraged to identify gaps and to come up with their own solutions for meeting these. Housing Corporation Innovation and Good Practice Grants should be made available to facilitate the development of new models.

"Filling gaps" could be by:

a) shared research and development by local RSLs to enable one or more to undertake a new activity

b) the creation of a joint venture, with different types of contribution from each RSL (e.g. loan security, cashflow support, revenue subsidy, seconded staff)

c) joint procurement to reduce costs

d) refocusing of activities (e.g. each concentrating on a different specialism)

e) development of a group structure

f) amalgamation or transfer of engagements.

In many areas, this methodology would be more effective if undertaken jointly by a group of local authorities that are co-operating on a regional or sub-regional basis on strategic issues.

The advantages of this approach are as follows:

a) It respects the independence of the RSL sector whilst equipping local authorities to be more active in the sector's management.

b) It builds upon skills and expertise already being developed in local authorities.

c) It gives a clearer role for local authorities that is distinct from that of the Housing Corporation.

d) Especially with the local authority playing an active "consumer champion" role, there is considerable scope for tenants and other service users to influence the strategy and its implementation.

The disadvantages of this approach are as follows:

a) In the end, it still lacks enforcement powers and relies on the co-operation of RSLs and the Housing Corporation.

b) It has the danger of lacking the "grip" of a directive model whilst creating a set of comfortable, cartel-like relationships with no real market or genuine choice.

c) It involves local authorities making complex judgements with long term implications without, at least initially, having the capacity or experience to do so.

A pilot project that is being developed by Birmingham City Council should provide important practical experience of aspects of the methodology described above. The City Council has been introducing arrangements that will enable the council to make a more systematic evaluation of the capacity of the sector. "Annual Partnership Reviews" are being used to profile and assess the work of RSLs across the City. The project has to date focussed on the activities of a small sample of RSLs, but the intention is to extend the approach. Whilst it has not been possible to evaluate the pilot for the purposes of this study, it will be helpful for any work to develop the methodology described in this report to take account of the Birmingham experience.

Conclusions and recommendations

There is in our view a strong case for suggesting that local authorities should be able to influence the shape and capacity of the social housing sector, in collaboration with other key stakeholders (including tenants and leaseholders and the Housing Corporation) as part of their wider responsibility for ensuring the effective operation of the local housing market. This is particularly important at a time when the sector is experiencing a period of rapid change.

However, it is important to place the issue of rationalisation firmly within the context of wider strategic housing objectives and the capacity of the sector to deliver these. Local authorities should not be seeking to impose any particular pre-determined blueprint upon the sector (examples of which were listed in chapter 2). On the contrary, in order to deliver the strategic housing role, local authorities should be working with consumers, RSLs, the Housing Corporation and other stakeholders to ensure that patterns of provision meet local needs. It is essential that diversity and pluralism of the sector are protected within any attempts to manage the market; indeed this is a central requirement of Government policy, and important to ensure that the sector continues to meet the needs of BME communities and those with special housing needs.

The most effective model for intervention is likely to be close to the "managed market" approach, although with some aspects drawn from the other two models. This would involve a more systematic approach to using the powers that are currently available, and would be based upon collaboration between local authorities, RSLs and the Housing Corporation.

Given the significant and increasing role that RSLs are playing in delivering local authority strategies, local authorities should be required (say) every 3-5 years to prepare an RSL sector "Expectations Statement" – detailing what is needed from the sector.

Together, local authorities and locally operating RSLs should produce a "Capacity Statement" identifying what the sector can deliver locally and how any gaps can be filled.

The Housing Corporation should provide funding for this process and act as "auditor" of the Capacity Statement. Local authorities should be encouraged to undertake this exercise jointly with other authorities where local housing markets extend beyond administrative boundaries.

Where conventional private sector guidance and enforcement is not judged by a local authority to be effective, local authorities should be able to support or participate in the creation of joint venture bodies with RSLs and others to improve standards and reshape supply within the private owner occupied and rented sector. The use of SHG (both local authority and Housing Corporation) should be widened to include the funding of these vehicles where the outputs will be housing either affordable to people unable to access housing on the open market or accessible to current social housing tenants.

Where these bodies require funding, authorities should be encouraged to use a range of funding methods appropriate to the business, including equity investment and loans.

To ensure that there is a local lever for effective management and to strengthen the local authority's role as consumer champion, RSL tenants should have the right to initiate a review by the Housing Corporation of the management of their homes by their RSL. This could be linked to the Best Value inspection regime. This would be triggered by a minimum number or proportion of an RSL's tenants in a local authority area demonstrating (by reference to the performance of the RSL) that the service did not reach an acceptable standard, and the RSL failing to address this satisfactorily within a given timescale. The results of such a review would be published, including any recommendations, which could include proposals for the management of the homes to be transferred to another RSL. An equivalent right for local authority tenants to initiate an inspection by the Housing Inspectorate could mirror this.

Appendix 1: Bibliography

Aldbourne Associates/Newbury DC/West Dorset DC (1997): *Vision into reality – The role of transfer authorities as housing enablers.*

Cabinet Office (2000): *National Strategy for Neighbourhood Renewal – Report of Policy Action Team 18: Better Information.*

CIH (1995) *Meeting Housing needs in the Private Rented Sector – Good Practice Briefing Issue No. 1.*

CIH (1997): *Local Housing Strategies – Good Practice Briefing Issue No. 7.*

CIH (2000a): Response to the DETR Housing Green Paper.

CIH (2000b): *Sustaining Success – Registered Social Landlords, Financial Risk and Low Demand.*

CIH/CML (2000): *Understanding Local Housing Markets – Their Role in Local Housing Strategies,* by Bob Blackaby.

CIH/The Countryside Agency/The Housing Corporation (2000): *Developing Housing Strategies in Rural Areas – A Good Practice Guide.*

CIH/LGA (2001): *CIH/LGA Briefing – Modernising the Legal Basis for Local Authorities' Strategic Housing Role.*

CIH/LGA (1998): *Designing Local Housing Strategies – A Good Practice Guide,* by Sue Goss and Bob Blackaby.

DoE (1994): Guidance for local authorities on the preparation of housing strategies.

DETR (1998a) *Modern Local Government: In Touch with the People.*

DETR (1998b) Guidance on local housing strategies.

DETR (1999a) *Modernising Government.*

DETR (1999b) Circular 10/99 – Local Government Act 1999: Part 1 Best Value.

DETR (1999c) *National Framework for Tenant Participation Compacts.*

DETR (2000a): *Quality and Choice: A Decent Home for All.*

DETR (2000b): *Quality and Choice: A Decent Home for All – The Way Forward for Housing.*

DETR (2000c): *Local Housing Needs Assessment; A Guide to Good Practice.*

DETR (2000d): *Low Demand Housing and Unpopular Neighbourhoods.*

DETR (2000e): *Responding to Low Demand Housing and Unpopular Neighbourhoods.*

DETR (2000f): *Best Value in Housing Framework.*

DETR (2000g): *2000 Housing Investment Programme.*

DETR (2000h): *2001/02 Housing Transfer Programme: Guidance for local authorities.*

DETR (2001a): *Local authority policy and practice on allocations, transfers and homelessness.*

DETR (2001b): *The Homes Bill 2001 – Housing Factsheet No. 8.*

DETR (2001c): *Local Strategic Partnerships – Government Guidance.*

DETR (2001d): The 2001 Housing Investment Programme Guidance Note for Local Authorities – Draft for Consultation.

DSS (1999): *Practice in the Administration of Housing Benefit – In-house report 55*, by Toby Taper, Trinh Tu and Ann Caughy.

HMSO (1987): *Housing: The Government's Proposals.*

HMSO (1998): *Bringing Britain Together; A national strategy for neighbourhood renewal.*

Housing Corporation (1999): *Best Value for RSLs – Guidance from the Housing Corporation.*

Housing Corporation (May 2000): *Regulating a diverse sector – The Housing Corporation's Policy.*

Housing Corporation (February 2001): *Developing the new approach to investment.*

Institute for Public Policy Research (2000): *Housing United: The Final Report of the IPPR Forum on the future of Social Housing.*

LGA (2000): *Vision into Reality – The Future Strategic Housing Role of Local Authorities.*

LGA (2001): *Research report 16 – Future Housing Directions: A survey of local authorities' strategic housing activities.*

National Housing Federation (1999): *Mapping the maze – The regulation of registered social landlords.*

National Housing Federation (2000): *Reaping the Benefit.*

Office for National Statistics (2000): *Neighbourhood Statistics Service.*

Appendix 2: Case study summary – The London Borough of Brent

Context

London Borough of Brent – Key Housing Facts (April 2000)

Local authority stock – no. units	10,918
RSL stock – no. units	11,806
Social housing as % all stock	22%
Private rented housing as % all stock (est)	17%
No. RSLs	56
No. developing RSLs	15
Difficult to let social units as % all stock	23%
Households in need on register	12,603
Council lets to new tenants per annum	512
Net council turnover	5%
Total RSL lets to new tenants/LA nominees	507
Net RSL turnover	4%
Homeless households accepted as priority (2000)	1,045
Priority acceptances per 1000 of population (last quarter year 2000)	2.8

(Sources: HIP Operational Return 2000, Housing Strategy Statement, DETR Homelessness Statistics)

Demographics and deprivation
- population is increasing, as are household numbers
- minority ethnic residents forecast to comprise 51.5% of population by 2001
- it is estimated that 13,000 – 15,000 refugees and asylum seekers live in the borough
- Brent was the 20th most deprived on the 1998 Index of Deprivation
- unemployment is higher than the London average, with concentrations in certain wards.

Demand and supply
The borough has areas of unpopular housing and considerable deprivation, but within a context of buoyant demand. The council forecasts a significant shortfall in the supply of affordable housing over next two years, based upon forward projections from the 1997 survey and the council's own administrative records (Housing Strategy Statement).

Areas of relatively unpopular housing include four communities that have been targeted for regeneration/stock transfer (Stonebridge, Church End/Roundwood, South Kilburn and Chalkhill), as well as a portion of the borough's sheltered housing (all of which has been transferred to a newly-created RSL which will finance a redevelopment/restructuring and refurbishment programme, described below).

The strategic housing role

Historically the London Borough of Brent has embraced the enabling role, and measures to intervene in and influence the private sector are a high priority within housing strategy. The principal driver of this has been the high level of housing need in the borough, and in particular the high incidence of homelessness, which has a direct cost for the authority. At the end of 2000, Brent had 3,488 households in temporary accommodation, the second highest figure in London (excluding households accepted as homeless at home) (DETR, March 2001). However, there are additional drivers for the influencing role in Brent. These include the authority's commitments to tackling social exclusion and inequality. Both are drivers for intervention, through regeneration activities and measures to meet the housing needs of the borough's black and minority ethnic communities. The authority is taking steps to establish a Shadow Local Strategic Partnership, and is in the process of examining how its role will develop within the partnership, and to what extent the strategic objectives of the partnership will become the strategic objectives for the authority. Both the council and the Shadow Partnership are grappling with the relationship between local democracy/council decision-making structures, and the governance of the Partnership itself. The authority has had an embryonic cabinet structure in place for over a year, running alongside a public service deciding committee. Further changes are planned to streamline the cabinet/committee structure, but there has been considerable local political debate about the most appropriate way to carry forward modernisation.

Cross tenure intervention

The authority has a well developed view of the importance of using its commissioning and statutory powers to intervene on a cross tenure basis to promote community safety and tackle anti-social behavior, harassment and discrimination. With SRB funding the authority established a mediation service in South Kilburn. This has since been extended to provide a borough-wide scheme jointly funded by the housing service, social services, the community safety unit and RSLs, and is available on a cross-tenure basis. The authority has been a pioneer in supporting the growth of black and minority ethnic (BME) RSLs, establishing strategies and targets for this purpose through its RSL Strategy (see RSL Strategy 2000-2003), and using a BME protocol to ensure that when mainstream RSLs act as development agent for BME partners, they provide this service in a manner that is transparent, fair and economic. The authority also directs considerable investment towards the private sector and new build in the RSL sector; of a housing capital programme budget of £12.281 million in 2001/02, £5m has been allocated for private sector repair grants and disabled facilities grant, £4.185m has been allocated as Local Authority Social Housing Grant with the remaining sums allocated to the Chalkhill project and HRA capital works. An approved development programme of £25 million is anticipated for 2001/02.

More generally, officers can foresee members wishing to develop the council's role as "consumer champion" and to use all available powers to influence the standards of service that citizens receive in all sectors. The authority already carries out a number of functions that sit well with this role. The authority has sought to exert its influence across the private sector, and in particular the substantial private rented sector. In addition, there has been some debate within the authority about an appropriate stance with regard to the RSL sector.

The social housing sector in Brent

In the past decade Brent has seen a rapid increase in the size of the RSL sector, partly because of the extent of RSL new build, but principally because of a succession of small-scale stock transfers. There are now more units in RSL ownership than council ownership, a fact which has prompted some consideration of RSL accountability. Members have periodically raised concerns about their ability to influence RSL activities, when approached by constituents living in RSL housing who have concerns about matters such as transfer applications or repair standards. There is a perception that RSLs are only truly accountable to the Housing Corporation, and that the levers of influence available to the council and tenants themselves are too limited in scope. This is an issue of significance in Brent both because a substantial number of council homes have already been transferred to RSLs through LSVT, and members wish to be able to represent these constituents' interests, but also because the authority is in the process of considering options for the future ownership and management of council housing.

There are over 50 RSLs operating in the borough, with 15 of these actively developing. RSLs fulfill a variety of important roles in meeting housing need in Brent. They:

- own/manage over half of the borough's housing stock
- are providers of new social housing for rent and sale
- provide a significant portion of the borough's temporary accommodation through private sector leasing and other initiatives
- contribute to private sector renewal through initiatives to bring empty private sector properties into use
- contribute to wider regeneration initiatives through partnerships such as Fortunegate, and Chalkhill, and through employment creation and training schemes (for example all developing RSLs are required to sign up to the Notting Hill Housing Trust Construction Training Initiative, and a builders co-op has been set up in South Kilburn to provide jobs and training for local people in partnership with and RSL and a local regeneration agency)
- provide the vast majority of the borough's sheltered housing and residential care homes (largely through Willow).

The local authority has traditionally sought to exert influence over the sector, because of the extent of dependence on (and investment in) RSLs to meet the council's statutory responsibilities and policy commitments (including housing the homeless, promoting the development of affordable housing by BME RSLs and promoting the economic and social well-being of the community through regeneration initiatives in all sectors). The authority has an RSL Strategy that sets out its objectives for the sector, and the standards and approaches that RSLs are expected to achieve. The authority exercises its influence through a variety of mechanisms including the borough's RSL liaison forum, Brent Housing Group, and the commissioning process for new build and other projects (such as temporary housing provision). The authority is in the process of conducting a joint commissioning exercise, in partnership with the Housing Corporation, to select partner RSLs to deliver the bulk of the RSL development programme.

Appendix 3: Case study summary – Manchester City Council

Context

Manchester City Council – Key Housing Facts (April 2000)

Local authority stock – no. units	54,340 (plus 9,500 outside area)
RSL stock – no. units	25,894
Social housing as % of all stock	42%
Private rented housing as % all units	11.5%
No. of RSLs	53
No. developing RSLs	10*
Difficult to let social units as % all stock	23%
Households in need on register	5248
Council lets to new tenants per annum	7,299**
Net council turnover (all stock)	11.4%
Total RSL lets to new tenants/LA nominees	1,965
Net RSL turnover	7.5%
Homeless households accepted as priority (year 2000)	2,908
Priority acceptances per 1000 of population (last quarter year 2000)	1.8

* Based on Approved Development Programme 2000/01

** Including 6815 introductory tenancies

Demographics and deprivation

- Ranked 3rd most deprived in the Index of Local Deprivation
- The economy is thriving but there is movement of economically active people out of the city
- Higher than average unemployment – 11 per cent. Economically active households account for only 56 per cent of Manchester population.

Demand and supply

The city suffers from rapidly changing demand for housing across all tenures. There is a lack of housing choice with limited supply of higher value homes, and no traditional suburbs. Seventy per cent of Manchester homes are in council tax band A.

The housing markets are failing in significant areas of the city, in particular there has been rapid decline in areas of pre -1919 terraced housing. Falling house values have led to poor quality and badly managed private renting, and rapid increase in empty homes. Social housing has "come to be viewed as a last resort". The region has the highest number of low demand private sector properties.

Understanding local housing markets

The main driver of Manchester's approach to the delivery of its strategic housing function is the recognition of changing demand within local housing markets. The enabling role is geared to the development of a cross tenure corporate strategy focused on the needs of the local markets and the intervention required at the neighbourhood level.

The council has been monitoring housing demand on its own stock since 1996, when the first steps were taken towards establishment of a Geographical Information System for the city, initially using information on council owned stock, supplied by area managers. In 1998, a study of demand in the RSL sector was carried out. The GIS system is now being further developed to improve city-wide intelligence on the operation of the private sector markets.

The system is used to generate ward profiles, using the toolkit approach developed by John Moores University, to examine a set of factors which contribute to the sustainability of each area based on a combination of individual property and enumeration level data.

The GIS is currently very housing-focused but it is also used corporately alongside information drawn from the City Atlas, a comprehensive guide to the city's facilities. A major feature of the GIS system is a web site which enables housing providers to view their information and obtain reports and maps, within the terms of a data sharing agreement.

Housing strategy process and consultation

The balance between the enabling and providing role is determined by the requirements of the local markets. Overall, there has been a shift in the allocation of resources towards private sector renewal – around 40% of the 2001/2 capital programme will be directed towards the private sector.

The council has a well-developed corporate vision for its strategic development work, particularly illustrated by the approach to setting the housing strategy. The council regards its Community Strategy, due to be launched in April 2001, as the framework for all corporate policy.

Strategy setting and review is undertaken on an ongoing basis at the Housing Strategy Corporate Review Group, attended by representatives at assistant director level from several departments including (as well as housing) social services, education, environment and chief executive's department. In this respect the housing department leads the council on its approach.

Consultation on the strategy is wide ranging, and representatives from all tenures are involved in the consultation process.

The main achievement in the development within the housing division of a comprehensive, corporate approach to strategic issues is that the underlying major issue of the state of the housing markets is high on the council's agenda, and is now driving overall economic and social strategy across the city.

Housing stock transfer

The council has an established programme of stock transfer where stock is owned by the city in other boroughs. 6000 units outside city boundaries have already been transferred to existing RSLs and a further programme of approximately 7000 is planned, subject to the necessary approvals and subsequent ballot, over the next two years. 6000 plus homes in Wythenshawe have been transferred to a new LHC at Willow Park.

The decision to transfer outlying stock was based on no continuing demand for overspill accommodation from within the city, improved accountability to those residents who could not vote for city council members anyway, and to make best use of limited financial resources.

The LHC at Willow Park has slightly less than 30 % representation by members on the board. The Housing Director is a board member. Because Willow Park owns nearly 90% of the stock in its area of operation, the LHC takes the lead role in co-ordinating the partnerships delivering the regeneration programmes in the area, and is encouraged by the board to adopt a wider role in non-housing activities. The council's perception is that the close working relationships between the LHC, council colleagues and members has enhanced the delivery of its corporate strategies.

Commissioning and RSL partners

There are more than 53 RSLs operating within Manchester, managing 27,000 properties. Joint commissioning is being piloted in three areas within the city.

The aim of the council's joint commissioning proposals is to achieve more coherent management at the local level, and the vision encompasses rationalisation of stock ownership and/or management, a reduction in the large number of RSLs operating in the city, and identification of lead RSLs who will actively develop and deliver regeneration proposals for their areas.

New East Manchester regeneration area

The council has been addressing the regeneration needs of the East Manchester area for a number of years. The vision of the cross tenure approach to regeneration work in East Manchester led to a successful bid for New Deal for Communities Pathfinder status in 1999, generating £52m of funding, together with a further £25m under SRB 5. This programme focused on 7000 households in Beswick, Openshaw, Clayton, Miles Platting and Ancoats. The development of the overall strategy for the economic and community regeneration of East Manchester is delivered through the Urban Regeneration Company, New East Manchester Ltd.

Consultation arrangements in East Manchester

There are a large number of forums through which local residents and partner agencies are continually involved in developing and reviewing the local strategy. The range of forums and working groups is continually evolving in response to issues identified for action and they are generally established in response to the wishes of the community to be actively involved.

There is no private sector landlords' forum for the area because private sector landlords have indicated a lack of interest in forming such a forum. The partnership is establishing an information service for landlords, and East Manchester will be a pilot for a mandatory licensing scheme.

Overall, the culture of the partnership and the area initiative is that the office is a public office and that an "open door" policy is operated. The effect is perceived as very positive in that the office is very well known in the neighbourhood and visited by a wide cross section of the community. It is acknowledged though that the open door policy is resource intensive, and can inhibit other work.

The office is occupied by staff representing estate management and the private sector teams, as well as the SRB and New Deal teams. The vision for the office is a seamless service to visitors and enquirers and the "open door " culture has helped to promote cross-tenure and joint working to the extent that this vision is beginning to be realised.

East Manchester is one of the three pilot areas for joint commissioning, where the four main RSL partners will each take the lead role as preferred partner in one of the neighbourhoods. In the longer term the council's current Options Appraisal exercise may lead to the creation of a new stock transfer vehicle in the area.

Supporting People strategy

The council's strategy for responding to their responsibilities under Supporting People has its roots in the well-established Corporate Supported Housing Policy (CSHP) which dates from 1996. The driver of the CSHP was the council's concern that supported housing was being developed across the city by RSLs and private landlords in a haphazard fashion, based primarily on the location of house types suitable for conversion/use as hostel accommodation. This was leading to concentrations of supported housing schemes in certain parts of the city, though those may not be where either the need or the relevant support services lay. Members felt this was in some cases having a detrimental impact on local communities and the residents of those schemes. The CSHP began as a set of key principles for development of all supported housing schemes in the city, and a requirement that all schemes should be assessed to ensure they met these.

Progress was initially slow and hampered by the lack of shared internal objectives and legal obstacles to the council's control of the supported housing "market". But Manchester's key principles have now been incorporated into the *Supporting People Policy into Practice* paper.

Appendix 4: Case study summary – The Welland Partnership and Rutland County Council

The Partners

The Welland Partnership is an alliance between five local authorities forming a rural sub-region of the East Midlands; East Northamptonshire District Council, Harborough District Council, Melton Borough Council, Rutland County Council and South Kesteven District Council. The partner authorities span four counties; Leicestershire, Lincolnshire, Northamptonshire and Rutland (a unitary authority).

The population profile and housing profile of each is as follows:

Local authority	Population	Population per km²
East Northants	73,079	143
Harborough	55,300	93
Melton	46,750	97
Rutland	34,600	88
South Kesteven	121,751	129

(Source: The Welland Partnership Housing Strategy 2001)

The aims of the Partnership are:
- to improve the quality of service provision
- to enhance arrangements for each council to comply with Best Value
- to explore the development of joint bidding/funding initiatives
- to explore opportunities for joint approaches to service delivery
- to encourage discussion and exchange of information between elected members
- to lobby all tiers of government and relevant agencies to promote the case for rural investment
- to adopt a co-ordinated approach in respect of rural service issues
- to embark on joint policy research where appropriate
- to increase participation and communications with market towns and rural communities.

The scope for achieving economies of scale through joint working and for exploiting the possibilities offered by information technology underpinned a number of the aims listed above. The relatively small size of each of the partner authorities, and their interest in pooling resources, has been an important driver of partnership strategy.

The rural dimension

The Partnership was formed to "give voice to the needs of this sub-region within the whole regional setting." (*Bridging Communities – A support strategy for rural life*, The Welland Partnership, undated). There is an explicit concern to ensure that the needs of the Partnership sub-region are not overlooked by funding and strategic planning agencies simply because the Partnership authorities do not share the characteristics of many of their East Midlands peers (because they have a combination of commuter belt affluence alongside pockets of rural deprivation). The Partnership was established at least in part to draw attention to the often hidden characteristics of rural poverty, and to develop and promote strategies for tackling rural deprivation.

Officers noted that a common characteristic amongst Partner authorities was a sense of distance from their respective counties; the sub-regional boundary makes more sense in many aspects of strategic planning.

Partnership structures

The Partnership is based upon a formal agreement (although not a legally binding contract) between the five authorities. The initial commitment was to establish a partnership group, involving members, who would meet at least quarterly, and report back to their respective authorities. As well as regular meetings between council leaders, there are monthly meetings of the five chief executives. Partner authorities are committed to developing and strengthening the Partnership, and expect a more formal relationship to be established over time.

The Partnership authorities are in the process of considering how best to move the Partnership forward. The option of establishing a jointly run board involving members is being considered. There has been informal discussion about how/whether this might operate as a form of Local Strategic Partnership, but little in terms of developing strategic directions.

Relations with regional partners

The Partnership is also still in the early stages of developing its relationships with external partners at a regional level. Key agencies are the Housing Corporation, the Government Office for the East Midlands and the Regional Development Agency and Assembly. The Partnership presents an administrative "complication" in that it does not sit neatly within the existing sub-regions used by regional agencies, which are:

- North Notts and Derbyshire Coalfields
- Southern (incorporating East Northants and Harborough)
- Peak
- Three Cities
- Eastern (incorporating South Kesteven, Rutland and Melton).

Welland Partnership authorities (and the RSLs interviewed for the study) are convinced of the relevance of the Welland sub-region, and are keen to see regional partners adapt to accommodate the group.

The Housing Group

The Housing Group of the Welland Partnership, comprising chief housing officers, has been meeting monthly since September 1999. The Group has, in accordance with the founding principles of the Partnership, focused on outcomes rather than processes, and has set itself "a demanding work programme" to ensure that meetings do not become "talking shops" (The Welland Partnership Housing Strategy 2001).

Housing Strategy

The Partnership developed a Housing Strategy Statement for 2001 largely to formalise the initiatives and work programme that the Housing Group had developed. This was felt to be necessary to demonstrate to potential funders that the Partnership has a distinct identity, and has the structures in place to deliver joint initiatives.

The Strategy is not intended to replace individual local authority strategies. It identifies the issues that are common to Partnership authorities as follows:

Welland Partnership Housing Strategy – Shared issues/objectives

Internal	External
Breaking down administrative boundaries that set arbitrary barriers to service delivery	Providing effective methods of service delivery in rural areas to support communities/tackle isolation
Working across Social Services and Health boundaries	Developing a voice for the sub-region to highlight the needs of the area/attract funding
Achieving economies of operation	Raise the profile of the needs of rural communities and the need for funding and other measures
Developing real and vibrant tenant participation	
Addressing the shortage of affordable housing	

(Source: The Welland Partnership Housing Strategy 2001).

Partnership initiatives to date have focused upon services to council-owned housing and the opportunities for pooling staff resources and intelligence within the Partnership, as the list of achievements from year one demonstrates (Welland Partnership Housing Strategy, 2001). In the coming year, the authorities plan to focus increasingly on joint approaches to identifying housing need, understanding the housing markets that operate in the sub-region, and addressing the need for affordable housing. Introducing new ways of working with RSLs to procure social housing is now a key work area for the Partnership.

In preparation for its new approach, the Partnership has worked with RSLs over the past year to establish a new liaison forum. This is open to all of the 31 RSLs that operate in the partnership area. Following an initial meeting, RSLs agreed to a Partnership proposal that a core group should be established involving six of the principal developing RSLs, who were prepared to commit resources to the development of Partnership strategy. Representatives of these RSLs now meet with Partnership officers on a quarterly basis, and key work areas are developed through sub-groups, which can be "led" by council or RSL officers.

One early initiative has been to develop a database of RSL stock and activities in the area, with all RSLs having been asked to submit a questionnaire detailing the profile and location of stock within the Welland area, waiting list and transfer list arrangements, rent levels, repair and management arrangements and tenant participation arrangements. The feedback from the survey is intended to assist with the creation of a database which will in turn be used to inform strategy. The key work areas for the RSL group include:

- progressing plans for the selection of preferred partners
- developing joint bidding/allocations on a cross border basis
- examining the scope for achieving common management standards
- examining the scope for a partnering approach to stock improvement, on a cross-border/cross tenure basis
- examining the scope for a common approach to allocations involving flexible lettings/greater consumer choice
- collaboration on tenant participation on a cross-tenure/cross border basis.

The Rutland context

Rutland County Council is a small unitary authority in the East Midlands region, which came into existence in April 1997 having formerly been a district authority within the County of Leicestershire. Key housing facts are as follows:

Rutland County Council – Key Housing Facts (April 2000)

Local authority stock – no. units	1372
RSL stock – no. units	240
Social housing as % of all stock	12%
Private rented housing as % of all stock (est)	10% (inc. est 3% tied)*
No. of RSLs	9
No. developing RSLs	4
Difficult to let social units as % of stock	3%
Households in need on register	187
Council lets to new tenants per annum	82
Net council turnover	6%
Total RSL lets to new tenants/LA nominees	22
Net RSL turnover	9%
Homeless households accepted as priority (year 2000)	6
Priority acceptances per 1000 of population (last quarter year 2000)	0.1**

(Source: HIP 2000, *Housing Needs Survey ** DETR Homelessness Statistics)

The authority is committed to maintaining a strategic housing role, but there is a belief that capacity to deliver all aspects of the role is constrained by the authority's size. The authority does not maintain a dedicated team to deal with strategic and enabling functions, and the Welland Partnership has provided an important resource for the authority in developing strategy. Were stock transfer to take place in Rutland, it is unlikely that the authority could sustain a strategic/enabling housing role. From Rutland's perspective, a more developed form of the Welland Partnership would offer a possible location for the function.

Other CIH Publications on housing strategy

Designing Local Housing Strategies

The dynamics of housing strategies are changing fast. There is a growing realisation that housing strategies must look forward, managing and influencing the local market place to ensure that everyone in a given place is adequately housed. This Guide will show you how to operate more strategically to involve stakeholders and engage local communities, to develop capacity and write a good strategy.

Price: £25.00   ISBN: 1 900396 96 3   Order No: 319   Published: May 1998

Understanding Local Housing Markets

This report is a review of a selection of housing strategies produced for local authorities, which claim to taker a wider view of local housing markets. It concludes that current techniques are not sufficiently developed and points to ways in which housing strategies could engage more effectively with private sector issues.

Price: £10.00   ISBN: 1 900396 59 9   Order No: 421   Published: June 2000

Black and Minority Ethnic Housing Strategies: A Good Practice Guide

This Guide highlights the need for positive action to tackle disadvantage and discrimination in housing. Based on a survey of all UK local authorities, it provides step-by-step guidance to help local authorities and RSLs work with key stakeholders and develop meaningful black and minority ethnic strategies that are linked to the local housing strategy. It looks at involving black and minority ethnic communities, aiming for racial equality in service delivery, working with other organisations and how to monitor the strategy's impact.

Price: £20.00   ISBN: 1 900396 64 5   Order No: 336   Published: July 2000

Developing Housing Strategies in Rural Areas: A Good Practice Guide

Guidance on local housing strategies does not always take account of the problems and opportunities in rural areas. This Guide will help local authorities to identify and address the housing needs of their rural communities across all tenures. Supported by the Local Government Association, it demonstrates how local authorities can develop more effective strategies which support rural regeneration and the creation of sustainable communities. A wide range of examples give practical ideas on encouraging the involvement of rural residents and implementing Best Value.

Price: £20.00   ISBN: 1 900396 84 X   Order No: 339   Published: July 2000

Sustaining Success – RSLs, financial risk and low demand

RSLs are working in some of the world's oldest industrial areas and are housing some of the poorest people in our society. Many are now major social businesses, with a responsibility to sustain communities and tackle social exclusion. This report puts forward proposals for how the government and the Housing Corporation can support RSLs·which may be adversely effected by low demand, particularly against the background of restructuring of rents. These include proposals on future funding, rationalising the sector and more flexible regulation.

Price: £20.00   ISBN: 1 900396 99 8   Order No: 423   Published: June 2000

Local Housing Strategies – Good Practice Briefing No 7

This Briefing offers guidance on developing, implementing and publicising a strategy and ways of consulting and involving other agencies at each stage. It includes advice on housing needs assessments and market analysis, rehousing, community care, council housing, housing associations and the private sector.

Price: £10.00   Order No: 59070   Published: March 1997

Modernising the Legal Basis for Local Authorities' Strategic Housing Role

A briefing paper from CIH jointly with the Local Government Association, arguing the case for new legal powers and duties relating to the strategic role.

Price: FREE

Prices do not include postage and packing. For more details, contact Publications Section, Chartered Institute of Housing, Octavia House, Westwood Way, Coventry CV4 8JP.
Telephone: 024 7685 1752 Fax: 024 7669 5110 Email: pubs@cih.org